The Evil That Lurks Within
*A Reluctance to Prosecute • Why You Should
Prosecute Dishonest Employees*
What the Troubled Company Can Do about
Crime
*Education, Prevention, and Control • Security
Management*
Confidential Information
Diversion of Company Assets
What You Can Do
Using Private Security
EPC Reviewed

Preface

This book originated from our idea to write a magazine article for entrepreneurs and managers on the 101 problems faced by troubled companies trying to stay alive. We hope we have not strayed too far from our original intention: to present a plain-English discussion of the major problems facing a troubled company, with concise solutions and examples from our own experiences and current sources.

I am fortunate to have worked as an employee for a wide cross section of American business. I have also been a consultant to businesses in many different industries. In 1991, I moved to Florida and undertook a turnaround consulting assignment with a company that managed seventeen casinos based on cruise ships. The company was severely troubled, both financially and operationally. The story of this assignment truly belongs in a Travis McGee novel. I was living aboard a 91-foot luxury yacht, which was the sole unmortgaged asset of the company's owner. Eleven years after working as a junior economist for the Federal Reserve, I was chief operating officer of the group of casinos and managed the operations of 3,000 slot machines and 200 gaming tables. My days were spent negotiating with potential investors and creditors, and my evenings and weekends were spent sailing on the daily casino cruise ships between Florida and the Bahamas.

It was in Florida that I met Jerry White, who approached the company as a white knight to refinance operations. Working together on land and on sea, Jerry and I built a strong professional and personal relationship which has continued to this day. It was during one of our shipboard conversations that we both realized the great need that managers and owners of troubled companies have for commonsense business advice on how to avoid failure. This book is the product of a year of writing, interviews with managers and owners of troubled companies, and conversations with colleagues.

We have used many of our own consulting engagements as sources for the examples in the book. With a few exceptions we have tried to protect the confidentiality of those involved by disguising the identities of the individuals and the companies. Any mistakes that we have made or stories whose lessons we have misconstrued are our own failings.

Matthew L. Shuchman
Aventura, Florida

Acknowledgments

First, I must acknowledge the support of my immediate family. My father and mother have been a source of constant encouragement, support, and welcome criticism that has extended far beyond what one should expect from parents. I am thirty-seven years old, and they are still interested in what I am thinking, reading, and writing. My sisters, Carol and Miriam, and my brother, Salem, have all sustained me with the emotional support that only close siblings can provide. They have all helped with their suggestions and critical comments on my experiences and writings.

Second, I must thank my friends who listened to my musings that one day I would write a book about what I was doing. Many gave me examples from their own businesses, and others read early drafts of the manuscript and gave helpful comments. Thank you NMB, DSS, JAR, SJB, ASM, CC, JB, PD, SK, PM, DW, JS, VSD, and BI.

To the more than forty employees of PCG, my first consulting company: Although the computer technology rarely worked as we expected, we learned to prosper. A special debt is owed to Stephen Schwartz, the first manager I trained at PCG. Together we learned how to work smarter instead of harder, and grew annual billings to more than $1 million.

Many years ago, I attended Joseph Mancuso's management seminar for entrepreneurs, given under the auspices of The CEO Club. The experience and Joe's prolific writings have had a strong impact upon my style of management.

I owe a particular debt of gratitude to my early and long-standing clients who placed their confidence in a young entrepreneur and from whom I learned so much more than I can say in this book through our conversations, occasional lunches, and by watching the way they managed their own firms. Thank you Jeff Tarr (Junction Advisors), Leonard Shaykin, Robert Shaykin, Michael Bruce, and John Quigley (Adler & Shaykin), Jack Nash and Leon Levy (Odyssey Partners), Ralph Guild, Vincent Bellino, and Pat Healy (Interep/McGavren Guild), Roger Phillips and Judy Robinson (H&R Phillips), and George Soros and Gary Gladstein (Soros Fund Management).

Last mentioned but foremost in my heart, I owe a debt of appreciation to Lisa F. L. Waterfield. As a casino executive, not only did she teach me about her business, but she has become my constant companion during these past three years. Each day, Lisa has listened to the stories of my current turnaround assignment or what I was writing about and reminded me that every reduction in personnel and every operation terminated represents names, faces, and families. She was the first to read the book, and it had to pass muster with her. Thank you for everything, but mostly for keeping me human.

M. L. S.

I would like to thank my family, most particularly my wife, Lilli, for her excellent typing and proofreading and my son, Hartley, for his computer and telecommunications assistance, which allowed me and my co-author to exchange chapters in minutes instead of days.

J. S. W.

To our new friends at AMACOM Books, Adrienne Hickey and Kate Pferdner: Thank you for having confidence in us and for helping to turn our manuscript into a book.

M. L. S.
J. S. W.

1
Introduction

In the United States, almost 100,000 companies will fail in 1994, 500,000 are troubled, and 1 million are having difficulties. Signs on buildings that advertise AUCTION TODAY, GOING OUT OF BUSINESS, LOST OUR LEASE, or ONLY ~~TEN~~, ~~NINE~~, ~~EIGHT~~, SEVEN DAYS LEFT have become common scenery. Many of these impending failures can be avoided. Even in the final stages of insolvency, a turnaround is still possible.

This book teaches executives how to manage for survival—rescue, rehabilitate, and turn around their ailing businesses. Each chapter provides a practical approach for accessing one class of problems and how to solve them using real-life examples and easy-to-follow lists of what to do and what not to do.

Who Should Read This Book?

This book was written for the managers of companies who are facing difficulty or possible foreclosure or who are asking themselves if they can afford the payroll next month. These managers are in the front lines of a troubled company's battle for survival and the book was written from their perspective. Using this book as a guide, many troubled companies can successfully avoid failure.

Anyone involved in business transactions with troubled companies will also benefit from reading this book: those contemplating an acquisition, liquidation, or sale; court-appointed receivers and trustees; and creditors. All will want to read this book to learn the strategies and tactics employed by troubled companies fighting to stay alive.

More than 1 million companies deliver less-than-average performance to their owners, shareholders, and creditors. These companies are in poor health and potentially on the road to being categorized as "troubled." Investors and managers of these underperforming companies can learn valuable lessons to apply to their companies by studying their sick cousins and reading about the recommended cures for the sicknesses observed.

Even managers at healthy companies will find reading this book worthwhile by applying lessons learned from studying troubled companies to their already successful businesses.

What Will You Learn by Reading This Book?

After reading the book, you will understand what can be done to "turn around" an ailing and troubled business. You will know how to use your position as a troubled business to your advantage when negotiating and learn the secret tactics others have used to stay alive. You will gain an insight into the thought processes and strategies used by failing and insolvent companies to avoid liquidation and renegotiate liabilities, conceal and sell assets, and maintain or disguise value.

As the manager of a troubled company, you will learn how to answer critical questions including:

- Do you have enough time to turn the business around?
- What can you do to reduce costs today?
- Can part of the business be saved?
- Who are your natural allies?
- Who are your enemies?
- Can you sell the business?
- Who would be interested in buying the business?
- Will filing for bankruptcy help to achieve your goals?
- What type of bankruptcy should you consider?
- Why is returning a company to profitability easier than you expect?

Each chapter discusses the business implications of a particular problem area. Managers will learn how to solve problems using real-life examples and easy-to-follow lists of what to do and what not to do. The examples in the book are drawn from our own consulting engagements and current sources.

Where bankruptcy or debtor-creditor laws may influence your company's course of actions, an overview in plain English of the legal issues is provided. Although the book is not a replacement for good legal counsel, it will educate the business managers or owners on issues to discuss with their lawyer.

How to Reduce Fixed Overhead

This book includes a step-by-step methodology with examples of how, without impairing the business, most companies can reduce their fixed overhead by at least *30 percent*. The book teaches skills for how to: negotiate with vendors, eliminate payables, reduce telecommunications costs, control and recover travel and entertainment expenses, and minimize insurance costs. Thirty percenting will be critical for all businesses competing in these difficult mid-1990s.

How to Reduce Personnel Costs

Chapter 9 examines the hidden costs of employees and how to control and reduce the spiraling costs of providing employee benefits. The manager contemplating layoffs of employees will read about the seven alternative methods of reducing costs without the need to fire anyone. Where layoffs are necessary, the manager will learn a systematic and humane method for terminating employees.

How to Reduce Real Estate Costs

For many companies, rent or mortgage payments can be the second largest fixed expense category after payroll. Chapter 8 explores methods the manager can use in reducing the costs of real estate, renegotiating lease and mortgage obligations, moving to a new location, closing unprofitable facilities, and subletting space.

How to Benefit from Media Attention

Effective public relations can be critical to a troubled company's future success. Chapter 12 shows how you can maintain and improve your company's public relations image even when the business is failing and how to use your image to help achieve your goals. Included are instructions on how to prepare and manage the publicity of adverse announcements.

How to Retain Customers and Collect Receivables

Troubled businesses often forget that their strongest supporters are their customers. In troubled times your customers can help your company to stay alive. Methods discussed in Chapter 6 include: how to get your customers to take care of your payables, how to collect and verify the company's receivables, and the secrets of finding hidden value in old receivables.

How to Sell a Failing Business

You may reach the conclusion that the best course of action is to sell the company. Selling a business is the one area most managers have no experience with. Selling a company that you are a part of is a skill that you can't learn in business school. After reading Chapter 10, you will know what to expect throughout the difficult emotional, legal, and business process.

Chapter 10 covers the complete process from locating potential purchasers to preparing for the closing. Using the many examples, checklists, and how-to sections, the reader learns how to write a sales memorandum, the seven places to look for potential investors, how to manage the due diligence process, and how to evaluate and negotiate with purchasers. Once you have secured a purchaser, you will learn how to move the candidate to a commitment and how to have a successful closing.

The Bankruptcy Option

Bankruptcy is discussed as a business strategy in plain English. Chapter 11 of this book covers the various forms of relief available under the Bankruptcy Code, including liquidations, reorganizations, and debt adjustments, with attention to both involuntary and voluntary filings.

After reading this chapter, business owners can use bankruptcy as an effective offensive or defensive business strategy. They will understand the relief available in bankruptcy, the impact on their business, and the pitfalls of filing without adequate preparation.

Although the book is written with a view toward managing a company to avoid bankruptcy, if your business would benefit from a bankruptcy filing or you are forced into an involuntary bankruptcy proceeding, then reading this chapter will enable you to prepare your company, your employees, and your customers to survive the bankruptcy experience.

Business bankruptcy topics covered include why most owners of small companies won't benefit from bankruptcy and the strategies for defending against an involuntary filing by creditors. Principals and business owners will find valuable the review of recent U.S. Supreme Court decisions that provide additional relief for small and medium-size privately held companies using chapters 11 and 13 of the Bankruptcy Code.

Preparing for bankruptcy includes understanding the implications of the court's definitions for insiders and affiliated businesses. This chapter teaches you how to protect insiders and affiliates from the wrath of creditors. The particulars of fraudulent transfers and preferential payments are addressed with attention given to how a company can avoid or repair these potentially calamitous situations before making a bankruptcy filing.

The search for bankruptcy counsel is a rocky road. After reading this chapter, business owners will understand who should advise them in bankruptcy and how to select a bankruptcy attorney. Techniques covered include how to make your bankruptcy attorney work for you and not for your creditors and why one bankruptcy attorney may not be enough for the closely held business.

Because it is not written by a lawyer, this book is unique in its sections on when you should not listen to your attorney and why some bankruptcy lawyers won't tell you the truth about business failures.

Personal bankruptcy for the business owner presents a group of problems that are unique to the relationship that exists between a closely held business and its owner. This chapter addresses the questions of: whether a bankruptcy filing for the business means that the owner will also have to file personally, how a personal filing may avoid a business bankruptcy, how you may be eligible to file again even if you have already filed for bankruptcy, and why most business owners should seek bankruptcy counsel independent from their business.

The strategic objective in filing for bankruptcy is usually to safeguard the future of the owners, the business, or both, even if bankruptcy means an orderly liquidation. This chapter addresses the future implications of a bankruptcy filing to the owners, the business, and the employees.

The Importance of Security to a Troubled Company

Most companies approach security benignly and react only when a problem occurs. But a troubled company may not be able to afford even one small theft, embezzlement, or breach of security. A company that is troubled is in greater need of security than at any other time in its history.

The discharge of employees, the closure of facilities, and the termination of operations that often accompany a turnaround present unique security problems. Chapter 14 addresses these problems and shows you how to proactively safeguard your company's physical assets, customer relations, and confidential information.

The reader will grasp the often neglected special security concerns of a troubled company. Chapter 14 includes checklists and how-to sections to help the manager immediately improve his or her company's program.

Is Your Company in Trouble?

For some companies, the signs of pending economic distress and future financial ruin are clear. Significant litigation by customers and creditors, frozen bank accounts, IRS tax liens, sheriffs at the front door, and notices of eviction are obvious signs. Diminishing sales combined with shrinking bank balances and increases in payables are also indicators to more astute observers.

Here are some examples of troubled companies:

- Companies that experience declining sales for several quarters without a proportional decline in the costs of operating their business are troubled and in a nosedive toward potential failure.
- A computer business that is too small to afford the costs of remaining on the leading edge of technology must make a decision soon or it will enter a troubled period.
- A retail clothing store with insufficient working capital to purchase inventory for the new season is facing very difficult times ahead.
- Insiders who drain a company's cash flow beyond what it can afford to support other ailing businesses may be choking the only milk-bearing cow they have left.
- Companies trying to maintain an image of success above and beyond what they can afford are troubled and accelerating their impending failure.

However, not all troubled companies exhibit obvious symptoms in the early stages of their affliction. A company can have money in the bank, be current on its payments to suppliers, be making a profit, and still be troubled. The impending loss of a major customer representing 30 percent of a manufacturer's revenues may not have an immediate effect on the company. The company may still show a profit for the year and have a strong balance sheet; however, the failure to replace the customer or reduce costs in short order will result in serious difficulties. This manufacturer, though exhibiting no immediate symptoms, is troubled and must take steps to secure its future.

How Did You Get Here?

A variety of causes can force a company into a troubled period. In the incipient stage the natural causes can include the loss of a major customer, the loss of a key employee, increased competition, the loss of a major product line or vendor, the failure of a planned expansion, or a simple decrease in gross profit margins. The causes can also be fraud, waste, mismanagement, poor accounting practices, theft, or embezzlement. The effect of any of these actions can cause a decrease in cash flow available to operate the business and eventually result in serious economic troubles and the potential failure of the business.

In the next stage the company begins to exhibit the effects of decreased cash flow. These can include a reduction of assets, loss of customers, departure of employees, loss of strategic vendor relationships, and loss of prestige in the marketplace. Credit becomes stretched to the limit, and creditors begin calling demanding payment. Vendors start changing payment terms from credit to COD and cash in advance. The company may become delinquent in paying some of its fees and taxes.

Rumors begin to circulate that the company is insolvent or facing bankruptcy. Vendors send final notices, and the company rushes to make payments to avoid repossessions and terminations of essential services. Longtime customers begin to question the financial viability of the company, and vendors refuse to do business with the company unless past accounts are settled.

In the final stages the company is usually insolvent. Litigation has been initiated by vendors and possibly customers. Legal fees become a significant part of monthly expenses. Failure to pay fees and taxes results in the assessment of penalties, interest, and tax liens against the company's remaining assets.

Vendors and creditors are harassing the company daily and refuse to be put off. Management must hide to avoid unscheduled visits by creditors. Rumors of bankruptcy are widespread. The troubled company exists as a shell of its former self and is unable to grow its revenues to sustain itself.

What Can You Hope to Achieve?

If any of the characteristics of a troubled company are familiar to your company's present illness, then don't despair. Even in the final stages of insolvency, there is hope, if the business or parts of the business are *viable*.

What are your goals? Is your goal to keep the business alive and manage the transition back to profitability or to scale down, reduce costs, and try to sell the operation? Are you trying to avoid the problems resulting from personal loan guarantees? Is this a family business that you hope will provide for your children? Are you over fifty and don't know how you would make a living outside the business?

What are your goals in trying to turn around your company? Why bother? You will make more enemies than friends in trying to turn around a business. Why not just walk away and start over? Don't start the rescue mission unless you have good reasons for undertaking the assignment combined with a realistic chance of success.

Without specific, clearly defined, and—most important—*realistic* goals, you are running a marathon without a final destination. Knowing your goals: (1) allows you to evaluate and select the best paths for achieving your goals and (2) lets you know when you have succeeded.

The Conflict: What Is vs. What Could Have Been

As a manager or principal of a business you may find yourself with the internal conflict between your images (i.e., your dreams) of how the company could be (if only you could get over this hump) and your company's present condition. When you are trying to return a company to profitability and financial stability, always strive to be a realist. Don't abandon your dreams of what the company could be. Do, however, put them on the top shelf and concentrate your present efforts on restoring your company to a solid economic footing.

Carefully assess all of your company's assets and determine what can be achieved with your current resources. Your primary mission is to stabilize your company's present financial condition and secure its future existence or prepare to sell it for the highest offer.

Money Won't Solve Your Problems

Most troubled businesses believe that a business loan or an investment of capital will solve their problems. Though money can purchase time to solve some types of problems, in most cases, money is not the underlying cause of a business's troubles and it will not secure the company's long-term future. The company may need additional funds to achieve certain goals, but capital is only *one* element of the recovery plan. Without a plan for recovery, additional funds will result only in additional debt and a further dilution of equity.

Courage Is More Important than Capital

It takes courage to write a plan for the recovery or the sale of your business. It is an admission that without the plan your business may fail. Don't forget that you are not alone in having entered a troubled period. Many of your neighbors and colleagues are in similar or worse straits.

According to Dun & Bradstreet, 87,000 American businesses failed in 1991, 96,000 failed in 1992, and almost 100,000 failed in 1993. Your advantage over these casualties is that you have recognized your difficulties and made your primary objective the charting of a course that will take you beyond the current troubled waters.

In some ways your business is unique. No other company is quite like it. However, you share many structural similarities with other businesses. Observing and analyzing the similarities found in other businesses will help you learn lessons to apply to your own company.

If you are a wholesaler, you can learn lessons from other wholesalers—both the ones that failed and those that succeeded.

If you are in the service business, you can learn from others in the service business, etc. A well-managed business is simply that: a well-managed business. Modeling successful practice is a useful approach.

There are many factors that contribute to the formula for success. Unfortunately, it is not always possible to determine why one company succeeds and why another company, using the same strategy, fails.

> It is not usually one large error in judgment or a wrong critical decision that leads to the failure of a business. More commonly the causes of failure are several small mistakes whose consequences were ignored or overlooked by the company's management.

This book, while focusing on the strategies for recovery and resurrection, examines the mistakes made by companies that led to their eventual failure. When managing the turnaround of a troubled company, you can learn more from observing the mistakes that other companies made than from trying to determine the causes of their successes.

Using this book as a guide, you can successfully avoid failure.

2

Managing Under Fire

Our original goal was not to write a book about turning around a troubled business but a book about business pathology, analyzing why a business fails and what managers and owners could do about it. The number of U.S. business failures quadrupled from 1979 to 1985, and net new business formation declined by 14 percent in the same period. Needless to say, because the country did not learn from the period's results, the rate of failure was replicated from 1988 to 1993.

Dun & Bradstreet's analysis of business failure from 1980 to 1990 shows that 62 percent of business failures are caused by various management shortcomings, from the lack of planning and controls to excess overheads and new product launch failure. Only 3–5 percent are caused by fraud, 5–10 percent by adverse economic conditions, and 5 percent by the inability to obtain new financing.

Business Pathology

We decided that a theory of business pathology—*The Art of Management Failure*, as we titled it—would not be the positive motivating text or panacea that management would be looking for. Therefore, to avoid our own failure we decided to look at the results of this mismanagement and produce a set of meaningful actions to save business from failure.

No Glory in Failure

There is no glamour or glory in failure. No magazine covers extolling your brilliance, no Baldrige prizes for quality, no after-dinner speeches at the Jaycees. Yet we can learn a lot from studying and analyzing failure. As with any pathology, it shows us what causes death and what to avoid. But American managers want solutions with catchy phrases that are simple, fast, and cheap.

The failure industry—corporate turnaround specialists—is relatively new and uninfluential. Few professionals want to be associated with failures, losers, and the pain and suffering of workouts, turnarounds, and retrenchments.

Dayton Ogden, CEO of one of America's premier executive search firms, Spenser Stuart, speaks of the lack of leadership talent to handle the challenges of the mid-1990's economy. What is needed is someone who can do more with less, communicate well, and make a profit. Most of his searches in 1993–1994 were for CEOs to take charge of troubled companies, including IBM.

Failure as a Right

Companies in distress are highly pervasive. While about 56 percent of companies manage to survive their first eight years, according to a study of 810,000 businesses by the New Jersey Institute of Technology, 44 percent do not. Fewer than half of the 1970 Fortune 500 are still around, and only 300 of the 1994 Fortune 500 will be around in the year 2000.

Failure is everywhere—as it should be in a free economy. One of the great rights of a free economy is the right to fail. After all, is it not the purpose of competition and competitive strategy to eliminate the competition to eventually get a 100 percent monopoly or at least a psychological monopoly in the customers' minds that only you can satisfy their needs with your products, services, or retail environment?

No Theory of Turnarounds

Any review of the literature in this field shows that there is no unifying theory of turnarounds, no common taxonomy or classification system or even a universally accepted lexicon of terms.

One of the authors, as a professor of management at three different graduate business schools in three countries, found that the concept of saving a business or even considering failure is rarely taught. Yes, there are cases taught of businesses with a badly launched product or poor distribution, but few business schools believe failure or its long-term solution is worthy of study.

The focus for the last thirty years has been on growth and strategy formation for companies in manufacturing with strong or potential competitive advantage. The company is always dealing from strengths with substantial resources, not from a need to survive or turn itself around.

Innumerable books have been written on the subjects of growth, mergers, and vertical integration, but not on dismemberment or business resurrection.

Business Has Changed

In the low-growth, low-inflation 1990s, things have changed. Nearly 80 percent of all businesses are in retailing and services. Business is global. Financing for small and medium-size business is hard to come by despite record twenty-year low interest rates.

Management experts now write of the failure of business schools to teach such relevant skills as leadership, communication, and entrepreneurship. The concept of teaching restructuring and downsizing was not necessary if there was unlimited growth. The conclusion appears to be that the preoccupation with growth is widely reported as the primary cause of corporate financial decline.

By 1990 economists were saying we were "overstored," "over malled," and "over factoried." For the first time since World War II, we have excess market supply over demand. Some 2.7 million white-collar managers have lost their jobs since 1989. Most are over forty, and have little likelihood of direct corporate reemployment. Office vacancies average nearly 17 percent across the United States, and industrial space vacancies sit at nearly 20 percent. There has been real price deflation in many product categories, and increasing prices to get a better cash flow from the business may no longer be an option. Growth in market share is not possible in many business categories with an older, more conservative customer base. Generation X is not optimistic about the next decade, and the Yuppies are now "Dumpies."

Survival and Resurrection

Retrenchment is defined as the significant reduction of costs, assets, product lines, retail locations, employers, and overhead. This book is not just about the process of retrenchment but about the concepts of turnaround: *survival and resurrection.*

Retrenchment is a component of the turnaround process—in a way, an operational reaction or response to financial decline and the failure of business strategy. The goal is the strategic generation of cash flow to bring the company back to profitability and to focus on the business segments with the best probability of survival and profit growth.

We have long been advocates of *logical incrementalism* instead of long-term strategic planning. Logical incrementalism requires us to learn from experiences and continuously and gradually change our strategies over time to avoid failure. But once in difficulty, being patient or trying to muddle through may not be enough. New strategies alone cannot alter the consequences of a hostile economic or competitive environment or the failure of management to perform effectively.

We disagree in part with John Goldhammer, in his otherwise excellent *The Save Your Business Book,* when he suggests that "No business difficulty is permanent. It will pass."[1] It will pass only when it is made to, recognized, and acted upon.

Most attempts to save a severely troubled business do not succeed. Only about 10 percent of companies in chapter 11 come out alive because the others don't understand how to utilize the bankruptcy process strategically.

As Richard Sloma suggests in his 1985 classic *The Turnaround Managers Handbook,* "Turnarounds also fail because they are initiated and implemented in the same manner and by the same people who allowed the firm to get into trouble in the first place."[2] We believe there is a process and methodology for the logical salvation of the business and procedures for its eventual resurrection. In *The Turnaround Survival Guide,* A. David Silver agrees that "there is a process for saving the troubled company just as there is a process for starting a company, or expanding a company, for buying a company, or selling a company."[3]

Mark R. Goldston, now famous for his revival of LA Gear, suggests in *The Turnaround Prescription,* "Businesses do not decline on their own; they are managed into and through the process."[4]

To understand the concept of *managing under fire* and turning around a troubled company, you must first understand what businesses qualify for the turnaround process, the severity of the problem, the difference between long- and short-term solutions, and the types of internal and external problems a business can face. *The Art of the Turnaround* is about the process and procedures of turnaround: survival and resurrection.

Turnaround = Forced Change.

Retrenchment is a competitive action that can reverse the impact of poor management. It is a basic strategy for companies that face eroding markets and declining profit margins. The process of retrenchment for the business is usually an essential element prior to implementing a new action plan.

3

Survival And Resurrection Planning

Lee Iaccoca understood what to do when he stepped into the troubled Chrysler Corporation. He recognized that he could not survive with a 2.1 million-car-a-year breakeven point. Chrysler had to become the low-cost producer; it had to close all unprofitable and antiquated operations, reestablish a market position based on product innovation, and reschedule and restructure its debt. Iaccoca established a two-part process: (1) survival (he cut his breakeven point to 1 million cars a year and forced creditors to reschedule his debt) and (2) resurrection (the K car followed by the Minivan and Jeep).

The recent demise of the thirty-year New York legal powerhouse Shea & Gould reflects a different pattern: the lack of evolution and change in a highly competitive market; no succession planning; money-losing operations in Washington that the firm seemed unable to deal with. High overhead and the lack of survival managers all added to the problems. Shea & Gould, a firm of more than one hundred lawyers, is no more.

Most experts felt Union Carbide's days were numbered in 1990. Sales had fallen from $9 billion in 1985 to $5 billion in 1990. CEO Robert Kennedy introduced a survival and resurrection plan to make Union Carbide the low-cost polyethylene and ethylene glycol producer. Kennedy cut fixed costs by 18 percent. Administrative expenses fell 27 percent in three years, and sales per employee rose 77 percent. To reduce his debt load Kennedy sold off all noncore businesses including such well-known consumer brands as Eveready batteries, Glad garbage bags, and Prestone antifreeze. Kennedy decided to focus on one business as a resurrection strategy just as the auto industry, Union Carbide's biggest customer, was taking off. The results: Operating income has risen 27 percent.

Iaccoca, Kennedy, and all other successful managers in a turnaround recognize that a two-step plan is needed in a severe situation. The first part is the survival plan, the second the resurrection plan.

The Survival and Resurrection Planning Process

Once you begin managing under fire, a planning process is needed. As an outsider brought in to effect the turnaround, you have about a week to get organized and about three weeks to put the plan together. Existing management has less time. You are the subject of scrutiny and calls to find out what you plan to do. Hasty action provoked by the need to be seen as doing something could be fatal. What counts is that you have a logical plan in place that recognizes the problems, their source, and severity, and that there are specific action plans in place to effect change.

At the end of each specific action plan you need to know who will do what, by when, and with what intended result. This type of action accountability is essential to the success of the overall survival and resurrection plan.

This is not a five-year strategic plan, which rarely works. It is a one-month/six-month/one-year program for survival and a six-month/one-year/two-year plan to follow for resurrection. While the resurrection plan may run concurrently if the cash flow and resources are present, there is usually a delay or time lag of three to six months before the resurrection plan begins.

Measurement and evaluation in a troubled business must be done on a dynamic basis. Either you have the cash to pay your bills or you go out of business. What are the cash consequences of all actions and transactions? Where are you at the end of each day and each week? Cash flow statements become your strategic survival guides.

Choosing the Turnaround Team

The moment the decision is made to produce the survival and resurrection plan, a team must be established to assemble the information, create the action plans, and formulate implementation and evaluation processes. This turnaround team is responsible for the plan's success.

Returning the troubled company to profitability usually involves terminations of operations and personnel. You cannot openly discuss these types of decisions with all of your employees, so choose your turnaround team wisely. Select as team members only the managers you need and those you can trust. For the most part, you should ignore company politics in making your selections. If the company is forced to close its doors, then politics won't matter. When effecting a turnaround you are unlikely to make any new friends, so don't try to appease individuals whose termination you may be forced to recommend tomorrow.

Candidates for the turnaround team should be independent thinkers, entrepreneurial, professionally capable, flexible in playing more than one role, and effective at playing on a team with managers who hold opposing viewpoints.

The successful turnaround team has a flat hierarchy with one leader who is supported by a group of implementors. Each implementor is responsible for a discrete area but should feel comfortable working with team members on areas outside of his direct control.

The Survival Retreat

With limited resources and a need to be on site to cope with fires, the management group has to get the job done in no more than three days of uninterrupted work. This means that careful front-end work is needed in gathering information and in structuring the time available—thirty-six to forty hours.

The optimal locations for this front-end work are away from the business. A nearby hotel or someone's recreation room is superior to the boardroom or office. Meals can be brought in and participants can stay overnight at the hotel. The Cosa Nostra called this "going to ground" when they were under assault by other gang families or the feds. Everyone got together under one roof and even brought mattresses with them.

In many urgent situations with medium-size companies and family businesses, we have "gone to ground" with teams in motels, summer cottages, and owners' basements. After three days of living in very close quarters, everyone was highly motivated to get the job done.

With large corporations we usually had the breathing space and time of at least a month. We started in the office for a week gathering files, followed by a weekend retreat at a hotel, then back to the office for two weeks, then again to the hotel for a further Friday-to-Monday final session. The survival plan that resulted was implemented while we worked on resurrection that included possible sale, mergers, and divestiture of assets. This usually took another ninety days before it could be implemented.

The Information You Will Need

Give assignments to each team member to bring the information needed for the discussions at the survival retreat. Tell each participant precisely what information she is responsible for and the amount of detail required. Put all information requests in writing and be explicit about the period and detail required. Don't assume that someone will know "what you mean." Most employees have little or no background in statistics and generate reports describing changes of .01 percent when the accuracy of the underlying information is + or − 1 percent. If you want figures rounded to the nearest $1, or nearest $1,000, then say so.

The Importance of Verification

Be certain that your instructions include a request for the manager to verify the accuracy of the reports personally. Often we have observed blatant errors in financial reports reprinted for months and sometimes years because of a lack of designated accountability for the contents of the report.

Throughout this book are warnings that information that has not been verified is useless in the decision-making process. Believe it! The company you are trying to return to good health did not become ill because of false or misleading information, but without *accurate* information, you will be unable to make the informed decisions that are both necessary and essential to turning your company around. Accurate information is critical to the survival and resurrection plan. Without it you are doomed to failure. If you are an outsider brought in as a new savior, be wary of what you receive and verify it for content and source.

Some information you need may already be available in your company's files. However, unless you are willing to verify the accuracy of the information, you are foolish to use it. Rely upon reports only after you have verified the accuracy of the information they contain.

The Usefulness of Certified Audits

Even information certified by public accounting firms should be viewed with suspicion. In several recent bankruptcy cases, charges of fraud and negligence have been brought against the auditors by trustees, shareholders, and creditors after they discovered "irregularities" in the historical financials of the bankrupt companies. Most of these cases have been settled out of court, but the size and frequency of these settlements are very disturbing to investors and creditors who rely upon "certified" audits for making business decisions to extend credit and make investments. Let's look at a few of these cases.

> *Warning:* Managers of troubled companies should be cautious about using any financial reports generated without their personal supervision.

In the case of the bankruptcy of Miniscribe Inc., a manufacturer of computer disk drives, Coopers & Lybrand agreed to pay $145 million to settle claims of fraud and negligence. In class action lawsuits filed in Texas and Colorado, the accountants, along with former Miniscribe executives and investment bankers in the company, were accused of fraud and negligence in the falsification of financial records that concealed the company's declining revenues. The plaintiffs alleged that Miniscribe had packaged junk computer hardware and common building bricks as marketable disk drives and computer parts. They claimed that Coopers was negligent for certifying the inventory and financial reports without verifying the information.

In the original case, filed in Texas, Miniscribe Inc., the company's former management, the investment bankers, and Coopers & Lybrand were all named as defendants. In 1992 a Texas jury awarded the plaintiffs $558.7 million! Coopers settled its involvement by agreeing to pay up to $50 million to the plaintiffs. In the Colorado case, the accountants admitted that Miniscribe had overstated its balance sheets for 1986, 1987, and three quarters of 1988 and eventually agreed to pay $95 million to settle their involvement.

Anyone who lived in New York City during the 1980s remembers the radio and TV commercials featuring Crazy Eddie smashing prices and holding "Christmas in July" sales. After the company filed for bankruptcy in 1990, investors and creditors alleged that Peat Marwick, the company's auditors, had been derelict and negligent for failing to detect any problems relating to the fraud, false financial statements, and overstatements of inventories. Although the full details of the settlement were not made public, in March 1993, the accountants, along with former corporate directors, agreed to pay $60.5 million to settle the claims arising out of the lawsuits.

In 1992, Phar-Mor, Inc., the discount drugstore chain, filed for bankruptcy and accused several of its former executives of masterminding a $500 million fraud and embezzlement scheme that may prove to be the largest in U.S. corporate history. For its alleged failure to discover the fraud and embezzlement, Coopers & Lybrand, which had regularly audited Phar-Mor since

1984, has been sued by the company's investors, shareholders, and new management.

Many involved with this bankruptcy case are questioning how the auditors could have been so oblivious for so many years. "This is basic accounting. This is auditing 101," says Paul A. Manion, Phar-Mor's lawyer. Phar-Mor says that the mistakes made by the auditors include looking no further than the cover sheets on detailed inventory records.

The allegations contend that the auditors missed it all. Manion says, "They virtually missed the entire company," and, "Some of the things that they failed to do are of the most fundamental nature." According to Manion, had the accountants investigated a little more, they would have found adjustments to inventory made without explanation. In its defense, Coopers argues that what made the fraud difficult to detect was the alleged collusion by the company's president and its top finance executives. David McLean, Coopers's associate general counsel, said, "Had we had any inkling that the senior management of the company was doing something fraudulent, we would have immediately expanded our audit procedures and dug deeper."

Leslie Fay, the well-known dress manufacturer, has also been the victim of poor accounting and auditing (only declaring a multimillion dollar profit for three years in which it had losses!) that put it into chapter 11.

> *Warning:* Business is especially vulnerable to the enemy within because most corporate auditing and accounting systems are unable to catch deception by those in positions of trust.

The cases of Miniscribe, Crazy Eddie, Phar-Mor, and Leslie Fay suggest that auditors don't always question the accuracy of reports and information given to them by executives of the subject company.[1]

What can we conclude about reports by CPA firms? Unfortunately, an audit is only as good as the information upon which it is based, and unscrupulous corporate officers or persons in

positions of trust can become very adept at methods of conceal-
ing fraud from auditors.

Professor Roman L. Weil of the University of Chicago's
Graduate School of Business, who teaches auditing, places the
blame on the auditor's training. Weil states that "the auditor
does have an obligation to keep its eyes open," but it starts out
"with the assumption that management is honest. So if management sets out to systematically fool the auditor, they are going
to fool the auditor."[2]

Joseph T. Wells, president of the National Association of
Certified Fraud Examiners, is much less philosophical about the
problem. Wells recently said, "Most auditors couldn't see a
fraud if it hit them right in the face."[3]

Although Wells's judgment may be too harsh, the recent
surge of fraud committed by insiders who successfully pulled
the wool over the eyes of trained groups of auditors certainly
says that auditors need to look closer and dig deeper. In most
of the previously mentioned cases of fraud, the procedures that
were followed were no different from those used at hundreds of
companies where no fraud existed.

Sources in the accounting trade, although not defending
their colleagues who were negligent in failing to detect irregularities, say that to verify all of the numbers that are required for a
certified audit would raise professional fees to levels that many
companies would be unwilling to pay.

The conclusion to be drawn for the manager of a troubled
business is that all reports based on information generated without proper supervision, or where the numbers were not exter-
nally verified, must be treated with suspicion. In a turnaround
situation there is very little room for mistakes in valuing assets
and liabilities and calculating the financial health of the subject
company. All information collected prior to the initiation of the
project should be regarded with suspicion until proved accurate.

Documents for Survival Planning

Exhibit 3-1 is a comprehensive list of the information that is recommended (i.e., desirable) for a first survival meeting. The doc-

Exhibit 3-1. Recommended documents for survival planning.

Origin	Description	Period
Accounting	Balance sheet (quarterly)	Last 4 quarters
	List of all business liabilities	Current
	List of all business assets	Current
	Income statement (monthly)	Last 12 months
	Cash flows (quarterly)	Last 4 quarters
	Cash flow projections (weekly)	Next 12 weeks
	Summary of outstanding taxes	Current
	Projection of outstanding taxes	Next 6 months
Personnel	All wages, salaries, and commissions	Current and due
	Organizational chart of the company	Current
	Company's personnel policy book	Current
Purchasing	List of suppliers and vendors	Current
	List of accounts payable (A/P)	Current
	List of disputed A/P	Last two years
Sales	List of customers	Current
	List of accounts receivable (A/R)	Current
	List of uncollectible A/R	Last two years
Executive	List of competitors and future partners	Current
Legal	Summary of outstanding litigation	Current
Warehouse	Inventory list	Current

uments are divided into groups by the department that should be responsible for the information. If some of the information is unavailable, don't delay. Hold the meeting anyway.

Reports from the Accounting Department

The accounting department is an important source for the compilation of reports necessary for making strategic decisions. Unfortunately, this department is also usually staffed by the lowest-paid (and often the most overworked) clerical employees in the company.

Although the balance sheet should encompass a list of all

business liabilities and assets, request a separate list of these items to corroborate the balance sheet and to identify areas for future investigation. Not all assets and liabilities appear on the balance sheet. This is either because they cannot be properly categorized or, in the case of related entities, the item needs to appear on the balance sheet of more than one company.

Business liabilities should include all accounts payable (A/P) and all scheduled debts such as loans, mortgages, leases, credit card payments, and utilities. Business assets should include all bank accounts, stocks and investments, real estate, vehicles, major equipment, insurance claims due, accounts receivable (A/R), deposits, and refunds due.

Both the lists of business liabilities and assets should be ranked in descending order and annotated with sufficient description that further investigation is possible without the need to consult the report's author.

The income statement should be generated using the most conservative estimate of revenues and the most liberal view of corporate liabilities. Too often we have seen income statements generated with hopeful projections of income rather than on the basis of prior history and common sense.

The most important of the reports that the accounting department is responsible for are the cash flow projections. These reports should be done with the most conservative inclusion of potential future income and with the most liberal estimate of future expenses. Ask for these reports as soon as you realize the company is in trouble. Don't waste time waiting for computer programming to generate these reports. Cash flow projections can be easily constructed by hand or using a personal computer and a spreadsheet package.

The summary of outstanding taxes should be divided into two categories: (1) corporate liabilities such as corporate income tax, state income tax, and municipal business taxes, and (2) trust fund obligations. Trust fund taxes are those taxes that the company collects as the agent of a governmental taxing authority. They are the most urgent taxes to pay because the directors, principals, and even the managers of the company can be held personally liable, and the liability is usually not dischargeable in bankruptcy. Included in the list of trust fund taxes are: sales taxes, payroll withholding taxes, Social Security, unemployment insurance, and workers compensation.

Many trust fund taxes become liabilities when the transaction being taxed takes place (i.e., payroll is earned or sale occurs) but are not due (i.e., paid to the government) until the end of the trimester or quarter. To encompass these potential obligations, you should request a list of all new taxes that are estimated as becoming due over the next six months.

Reports from the Personnel Department

The report of all wages, salaries, and commissions (see Exhibit 3-2) is one of the essential elements in examining the costs savings that could be realized by terminating or reducing operations. The report should include the full monthly cost of each employee or regular consultant and independent contractor. In addition to salary and taxes, full cost includes any regularly paid benefits such as health and life insurance, car allowances, hous-

Exhibit 3-2. Report of all wages, salaries, and commissions.

Name	Monthly Gross Salary	Health and Life Insurance	Auto and Other Benefits	Taxes, SS, SUI, and WCI*	FULL MONTHLY COST	Percent Share
Joe	$ 4,000	$ 400	$500	$ 600	$ 5,500	31
Sally	$ 3,000	300	200	450	3,950	22
Tom (consultant)	2,500	0	0	375	2,875	16
Jim	2,000	200	0	300	2,500	14
Jill	1,500	150	0	225	1,875	10
George	1,000	100	0	150	1,250	7
TOTALS	$14,000	$1,150	$700	$2,100	$17,950	
	78	6	4	12	Percent Share	

*Taxes = city and state payroll taxes; ss = employer's Social Security contribution; SUI = state unemployment insurance; WCI = workers compensation insurance.

ing allowances, educational benefits, and commissions. The report is most useful if ranked in order of descending total compensation.

The second report provided by the personnel department is an organizational chart of the company. Although organizational charts generated by the personnel department may be of limited usefulness, they provide a starting point for the team to work with. Last is the company's personnel policy book. This is important because it states the company's policy on retirement, termination, and severance. The team needs this information when estimating the cost of terminating or reducing operations. If the company doesn't have a written policy on personnel, then the limitations are those state and federal regulations that apply to your industry and any contracts with employees (union or individual).

Reports from the Purchasing Department

The list of major suppliers and vendors should include a brief description of each supplier including products or services purchased, payment terms, amounts past due, and disputes about shipments. The report should also include at least one alternate supplier for each major purchasing category.

Though the list of accounts payable would normally come from the accounting department, without the annotations of those responsible for purchasing, the report lacks the required detail. Ask the purchasing department to annotate both the current A/P list and the list of disputed A/P. Both lists should be ranked in descending order of the outstanding balances along with aging information for each account.

Reports from the Sales Department

The sales department should provide a complete list of all customers who have done business with the company during the past year. The department should obtain a copy of the accounts receivable reports from the accounting department and annotate it as required, just as in the purchasing situation for accounts payable.

Where an account is listed as uncollectible or disputed, the sales department should be required to provide additional information as to the circumstances surrounding the problem and any potential resolution. Specify that you want to know about any inventory that is at a customer site on a provisional, loan, or trial basis. All lists should be ranked in descending order of the outstanding balances along with aging information for each account.

Reports from the Executive Branch

The lists of competitors and future potential partners will be required to explore candidates for sales of inventory, outplacement of employees, and potential investors in your company. Included in your list of current competitors should be both your friends and your adversaries. As long as the price is right, why should you care if the purchaser was formerly a bitter enemy? The list of potential partners should include related businesses and firms in the same business in different geographic or discrete markets.

Reports from the Legal Department

Either your inside legal counsel or the person responsible for managing the company's outside counsel should write a brief summary of all outstanding litigation, arbitration, judgments, and proceedings in which the company or its principals are involved.

Reports from the Warehouse

Although the accounting department should have a list of the company's inventory, we rarely trust these reports. The staff of the warehouse is usually more knowledgeable than management as to the quantities and condition of goods in the warehouse. Choose a trusted manager to oversee a spot inventory of all goods in the warehouse and in other storage facilities.

This basic collection of information is the core of the survival plan. It helps you cut your costs and improve survival cash. The turnaround team should be able to formulate plans based on the detailed analysis for each business segment we provide later in the book.

Resurrection Planning

Once the business survival plan has been established you can then proceed to think on a long-term basis. The basic fire is out. Now is the time for entrepreneurial change, asset disposition, strategic partnerships, and repositioning of the business for the long term—the next six months to two years. (In later chapters we deal in greater detail with asset disposition as well as the sale of the business.)

The basic planning model and process for resurrection is not unlike that given for survival. You gather facts, prepare for a retreat, assemble the team, analyze the information, and prepare an action plan with specific responsibilities and time frames.

Documents Needed for Resurrection Planning
- Previous year's strategic plans and budgets
- List of all stores, offices, warehouses, and locations
- List of leases
- Detailed list of competitors with evaluation of strengths and weaknesses
- Marketing plans
- List of all products, costs, product lines sold, and institutional agreements
- All advertising and promotion copy
- List of major customers and suppliers
- Any current consumer or market research
- List of key personnel
- Industry or sector data on growth and trends

Analyzing the Business

There are many ways to examine the business. One way is to divide the company into operational areas and then draw a functional segmentation diagram. Using the segmentation, it's a straightforward process to take the information from the financial reports and perform a preliminary analysis of the profitability of each segment. Using profitability as a guide you can begin making decisions on which areas to concentrate your efforts upon.

To analyze the profitability of each segment you need to determine which segments are responsible for expenses and which are responsible for revenue. Although at first glance it would appear that most businesses already know where their revenue comes from, our experience has shown otherwise. An early rule to follow in managing a troubled company is to discard your first assumptions. Most companies know where their gross revenues come from but are not infrequently mistaken about the net profit derived from each segment or division.

Segregate the business into distinct and functional areas. The company may already be divided into different departments, groups, or products, depending on your type of business. In constructing a model of your company the differentiation by function is the most important (i.e., at the top level of the hierarchy).

Building a Functional Model of Your Business

All businesses, even those with only one employee, have different functional areas. Each employee in a small business may wear more than one hat (i.e., perform more than one function), and in a large company, more than one person may wear the same hat. Both large and small companies can be divided into functional operational areas.

Exhibit 3-3 shows examples of two businesses that have been divided into functional areas. We call this mode of analysis the functional segmentation of a business. The examples are a service business (which could be a carpet cleaning business or a professional organization such as a medical, legal, or accounting practice) and a product distribution company. Exhibit 3-4 expands upon the functional segmentation of the product distribution company. In this example, purchasing is the primary category under which three types of purchases are made: new products, existing major product lines, and service parts and supplies for the company. The functions of the sales, service, accounting, and warehouse departments have also been expanded upon in the same way.

Exhibit 3-3. Examples of functional segmentation.

SERVICE BUSINESS

Producers	Sales	Administration

PRODUCT DISTRIBUTION COMPANY

Purchasing	Sales	Service	Accounting	Warehouse

Exhibit 3-4. Expanding upon the functional segmentation.

PRODUCT DISTRIBUTION COMPANY

Purchasing

New Products	Major Products	Parts and Supplies

Sales

Inside	Foreign	Major account	Outside

Service

Inside	Outside	Inside

Accounting

Accounts receivable	Accounts payable	Payroll and personnel	General ledger and taxes

Warehouse

Used equipment	New equipment	Supplies

Assessing the Profit Contribution Analysis of Each Segment

The next step is to examine the operations of the company and directly allocate for the last year (or at the least, the most recent six-month period) the expenses incurred and the revenues received by each functional area (segment). Use the financial documentation that you prepared for the meeting as the source for this information.

Allocating Expenses

For some categories of expenses, such as the payroll cost of a salesperson, allocating the expense to one category is a simple task. For other categories, such as the cost of the company van (used by the purchasing, service, and warehouse departments), attributing the cost to one department is not possible. Where it is not possible to allocate the entire expense item to a specific operation at the second level, then allocate it to a primary function and apportion it later.

Some expenses, such as utility costs (telephone, electric, water, gas, etc.), are difficult to allocate even at the primary level. Attribute these costs to general overhead. Later you can apportion these general overhead costs into prorated portions for the primary and secondary levels.

Allocating Revenues

Perform the same exercise you did for dividing expenses to attributing your company's revenues. Don't worry that your service department has no revenue and only expenses. You can insist that without a service department you wouldn't have any sales. But the purpose of the exercise is not to decide which departments to eliminate, only which areas require the first attention.

Allocating General Overhead

When it is difficult to allocate the full amount of the revenue or expense to one functional segment, use another expense or revenue category as a guide to how to divide it between more than one segment. For example, you may find it difficult to divide the utility costs between the accounting and the purchasing departments. However, you know that purchasing occupies only 1,000 square feet of a 10,000-square-foot office building and accounting occupies approximately 3,000 square feet. To apportion utility costs, attribute 10 percent of the utility bill to purchasing and 30 percent to accounting.

Conducting Turnaround Team Discussion

Gather the turnaround team and discuss the results of your analysis. Your aim is to direct discussion toward two important issues:

1. What business are we in?
2. What business do we want to be in?

What Business Are We In?

There is more than one way to answer this question. One approach is to access where the company's efforts are devoted where:

$$\text{Efforts} = \text{Capital} + \text{Labor} + \text{Management attention.}$$

For example, an automobile dealership that devotes 75 percent of its overhead and most of its management attention to a truck sales division that generates only losses may view itself as being in the business of selling trucks, even though it derives its profits elsewhere.

Another approach, preferred in the turnaround scenario, is to examine the net revenue attributed to each functional area and rank the areas in order of descending revenues. You may believe that you are in the business of *selling* new lawn mowers until you discover that more than half your net revenues are derived from your *servicing* of used mowers, not selling new mowers.

What Business Do We Want to Be In?

Now consider the question "What business do we want to be in?" One choice is the business that is best for you on a personal basis, another is the business that is best to be in during this recovery period, and then there is the choice of the business you desire to be in for the future.

Is each sector of the business profitable? A response that the service department is unprofitable but without it you couldn't sell new equipment is improper at this juncture. If someone were to tell you that you could operate only one department and your objective was to retain the most profitable area, what would you keep?

Considering the Company's Options

Now that you are in the midst of resurrection and have improved cash flow and some financial stability, the company can consider more options and alternatives. The planning process will identify the optimal routes to follow. These may include many repositioning strategies plus the eventual sale of the business or its component parts. During the option generation process, you can assess new directions for the business, whether new management staff is needed, and whether you believe the business is viable in the long term.

Twenty Rules to Remember When Managing Under Fire

1. Your first assumptions are usually incorrect.
2. Support management decisions by collection of data and analysis, not by relying on old maxims.
3. Don't rely upon information that cannot be verified.
4. Never minimize the magnitude of an expense or the benefits of a cost reduction without measuring it.
5. There are no "fixed" expenses. "Fixed" means only that you can quantify the expense before renegotiating it.
6. If maxims are used around your company to explain or justify decisions, be certain that these maxims are representative of your corporate image and philosophy.

7. The cardinal rule of the troubled company when negotiating is: If those you do business with will benefit more by your staying in business than by your closing, then you have leverage and should use it.
8. Even when managing under fire, the standard rules of good management still apply.
9. Don't model management's behavior upon Arnold Schwarzenegger's portrayal of a futuristic hit man in *The Terminator*. Don't try to imitate Jimmy Stewart in *It's a Wonderful Life*, either.
10. A good manager should be effective, efficient, and compassionate, yet remain firm when executing decisions.
11. Only children like surprises. Nobody in business likes surprises.
12. Your current counsel (accountants, lawyers, and consultants) are probably not qualified to give you advice when facing economic failure or insolvency.
13. Use professionals only for their specialty.
14. Be ever vigilant of and conscious of conflicts of interest.
15. Confirm all "understandings" in writing.
16. You have no true friends in business. Your "friends" are primarily in business to make a profit. Friendship is secondary.
17. The best forms of payment are cash, cashier's check, or certified check, in that order.
18. First you must ensure your survival. Second you work on the plan for resurrection.
19. The 30 percent rule applies to nearly any business. All costs when reduced by "30 percenting" yield survival numbers.
20. Look to see if cost centers can be made into profit centers.

Notes

1. Jay Greene, "Accounting Firms Question Their Role as Detectives," *The (Cleveland) Plain Dealer*, April 4, 1993, p. E5.
2. Ibid.
3. Ibid.

4
Reducing Overhead

To reduce expenses the best advice is: Stop spending money! Cash is king, and right now your company needs every bit of cash to survive. Reducing expenses is not a project for one day, it's a philosophy of business. We agree with management guru Peter Drucker who said, "Absorption of overhead is one of the most obscene terms I have ever heard."

Do not permit yourself to speak in terms of an Accounting 101 phrase like "the amount of overhead that can be supported by the current business." The only amount of overhead that a company should "support" are those expenses that are *absolutely* necessary for the business to be profitable. Any other expenses are luxuries and fringe benefits. For tax purposes, we may call these extraneous expenses overhead, but we all know they are luxuries and unnecessary.

Managing for Survival vs. Managing for Success

Before your company became immersed in troubled waters you were managing for success and your objective was to maximize the long-term prosperity of the business. Now you are managing for survival and your objective is to keep the company's head above water and chart a course that will stabilize the company's future financial position.

You are not downsizing your company, but—in the terminology of the 1990s—you are rightsizing your company. The business should never have become encumbered by expenses that are unnecessary to make a profit.

While trying to rightsize your company, you may not actually reduce true overhead. You can, however, reduce the list of expenses that are treated as overhead and then eliminate or curtail these unnecessary expenses.

What Do You Really Need to Survive?

As the manager of a troubled company, the questions you must ask every day are "What does the business really need to survive?" and "How can I stretch my cash flow to get the production out the door?" With this in mind, examine the regular expenses that your company incurs and determine if anything can be done to reduce them.

As a senior manager, you are unlikely to know all of the areas where waste occurs. Your junior managers and the troops, however, always know where the excesses are. You don't need to teach your employees how to reduce costs. They already know how. What you must do is inspire in your employees the philosophy that reducing costs is necessary for the company to remain competitive, stay in business, and protect their jobs.

Senior management must set an example. Don't be a skinflint, but try to set the example that everyone can economize. Driving a new Mercedes to work and then lecturing managers on the urgent need to reduce costs isn't likely to be very effective.

> In a turnaround, there are no fixed expenses. "Fixed" means only that you can quantify the expense before reevaluating your needs or renegotiating the costs.

The list of expenses that should be examined for possible reduction or elimination is different for each type of business. The following list details a few general areas where cost savings can be found. Some are discussed in detail in this chapter.

Expenses to Reduce or Eliminate

Airline tickets	Maintenance contracts	Subscriptions
Auto rentals	Office supplies	Taxicabs
Beverages	Overnight couriers	Telephones
Company food	Packing materials	Transportation
Education	Parts	Travel
Hotels	Photocopying	Utilities
HVAC (heating, ventilation, air-conditioning)	Postage	Vacation days
Landscaping	Shipping	Vehicle maintenance
Laundry	Sick days	Waste removal

Reducing Expenses by 30 Percent

Although each troubled company is different, by carefully examining all areas of the company's operations, turnaround managers will discover that a savings of *30 percent* of expenses is realizable. Some turnaround experts will tell you to cut expenses until it hurts and then cut some more. This chapter will detail many ways to reduce expenses without the pain. By instilling a philosophy of conservation and managing for survival, management can achieve 30 percent reductions in the level of expenses without inflicting trauma upon the surviving employees.

Making Managers Accountable for Expenses

One way to start the process of cost reduction is to make each manager responsible for, and *accountable for,* the expenses of his area. Explain the new agenda to each manager. Expenses that are not necessary cannot be tolerated. The company must remain strong and competitive. Assure the staff that no one will be punished for past excesses but that each department will be without question responsible and accountable for its own expenses.

Request from the accounting department a list of all the expenses of the company for the past three months divided by department or by function. Review this list with each manager in a meeting that includes other managers. Ask the responsible managers for their input on how they plan to reduce costs in their areas without curtailing production or efficiency.

Don't overmanage the meeting. Give your managers free rein to suggest even the most ludicrous ideas, and then discuss the ideas as a group. You may discover that your own lieutenants can solve problems in hours that you have wrestled with for months.

Assure the managers that the exercise is not intended as a punishment for past sins (of management or employees) or as a witch-hunt for any one employee. The objective is to teach responsibility and *accountability* for costs at all levels of the company. If the exercise is performed with the proper attitude, you should gain a valuable insight into the areas where the company can reduce expenses.

Making Auditing the Responsibility of Each Manager

Request that each manager carry the lessons learned back to the employees who report to her. The message is that the company must have responsibility and accountability for costs at all levels.

Each manager should explain the following to each employee:

> "Overhead has grown to include costs and expenses that are not necessary for the company to operate. The new agenda is to identify these areas and reduce the excess and the waste. The results will help the company to remain competitive and to overcome its current difficulties.
>
> "We must all work together as a team to examine all of the costs and expenses of our department and consider the ways in which these can be reduced."

Each manager should arrange to meet with her employees at least once a week for the first month. Employees should be assured that there is no intent to punish anyone for past excesses or other sins.

Managers must be frequently reminded that the objective of the exercise is to teach responsibility and accountability for costs at all levels of the company.

Four Steps to Reduce Expenses

1. Meet with your managers and review, as a group, the current list of expenses for each department that are treated as overhead. Obtain their input on what expenses can be eliminated or curtailed.
2. Inform your managers that they are responsible and accountable for the expenses of their areas.
3. Let your managers know that they must carry the message back to their employees and work their departments as a team to carry out the mission.
4. Meet once each week with the group of the managers to review the costs savings. Each time an expense is identified that can be eliminated or curtailed, a schedule should be agreed to for realizing the costs savings.

The Problem of Chargebacks

When the cash flow of a company is limited, the company can be strangled by the embedded costs of doing business. For a service company these costs can include shipping, messengers, taxi services, and long-distance telephone charges. For a distribution or manufacturing company these costs can include freight, packaging, trucking, and insurance.

It is standard practice to incur these charges and then invoice the customer for the costs of the services. These costs are called expenses, handling, shipping charges, re-bills, or chargebacks. Some companies add a fixed percentage of profit or overhead to the cost before invoicing the customer. The advantage of accepting responsibility for the direct costs of these services and then invoicing the customer is the profit gained by inflating the additional overhead charged.

Service companies are perpetually concerned with overhead that is not attributable to a particular client. Those businesses that are not concerned with these types of cost should be. The case is not uncommon of the office manager trying to play detective after totaling the Federal Express bills only to discover that thousands of dollars a year of overnight packages were being sent by the company without the costs being re-billed to the proper customer.

Product-based companies are not exempt from these types of problems. Annual freight bills for tens or hundreds of thousands of dollars that were not re-billed to customers can significantly decrease a company's profits.

The general problems with chargebacks are primarily that: (1) they have a bad habit of growing more rapidly than the underlying revenue and (2) those that are not or cannot be re-billed to customers become overhead to your company. Specifically, chargebacks are problems for a troubled company because:

- The company is responsible for the charges.
- They increase your accounts payable.
- The tracking and rebilling of chargebacks are a bookkeeping nightmare and require extensive manual paperwork.
- The rebilling becomes part of your company's accounts receivable and is subject to the same delays in being paid that your invoices normally receive.
- If your customers are experiencing financial troubles, you may be incurring a receivable of questionable value.

The Solution to Chargebacks

The easy solution to most of the problems attributable to chargebacks is to not have the costs billed to your company. Why use your company's credit when you can grow your business on your customer's good credit? Using your customer's direct billing accounts reduces your accounts receivable and your accounts payable attributable to chargebacks and does not drain your company's cash flow.

Direct billing also eliminates a significant portion of the

bookkeeping chore of tracking and re-billing expenses attributable to each client and usually reduces client inquiries about the service costs associated with chargebacks.

The more economically distressed your customers, the more important it is to use their charge accounts where possible and not your company's credit.

A Service-Based Example

At a consulting firm that was experiencing a cash flow shortage, chargebacks accounted for one-third of the bookkeeper's time and could represent as much as 25 percent of the firm's A/R. The firm was being confronted with payables that were overdue and chargebacks that had not been invoiced to clients. Compounding the problem, its overnight courier accounts and its travel agency (mostly used for chargebacks) were both calling daily regarding overdue payments. The firm was more than three months behind in allocating and re-billing chargebacks, and yet the providers wanted to be paid or they would terminate service.

The problem was solved when, after consultation with major clients, the firm began using the clients' courier accounts (Federal Express, UPS, DHL, etc.) when sending overnight packages. It also began using the prepaid airline tickets and hotel arrangements provided by the clients' travel agencies. It even started using the clients' credit cards when making long-distance telephone calls on their behalf.

Although the solution did not entirely eliminate chargebacks, it resulted in a reduction of at least two-thirds of the value of outstanding chargeback invoices and more than half of the volume.

The solution was a win-win-win for the troubled company, its customers, and its vendors. The troubled company was able to continue providing services without the threat of interrupting service for want of an airline ticket or messenger; the customers were pleased because they knew exactly what they were paying for; and the vendors were pleased because they were being paid.

A Product-Based Example

A manufacturing company had fallen behind in paying its
freight carriers. The carriers refused to pick up shipments until
past accounts were settled. The company had orders ready to
ship but no way to deliver them to the customer.

After being honest with one customer, the manufacturer
found a solution. The customer told the company to use its accounts with the same carriers. The manufacturer quickly discovered that many customers were willing to let it use their
shippers and pay directly for any costs incurred. The solution
was a win-win for both the manufacturer and its customers.

*To reemphasize, the easiest method of solving most of the problems
attributable to chargebacks is to not have the costs billed to your
company.*

Reducing Travel and Entertainment Expenses

Travel and entertainment (T&E) are expense categories into
which many unrelated expenses are often allocated. It is also
surprising how few companies spot-check or audit the expense
reports submitted by their employees. Unaudited T&E offers a
great opportunity for abuse and overspending, and its reengin-
eering can account for up to 20 percent of cash savings in a turnaround.

Auditing expense reports does not assume that you have
dishonest employees, but the results help in identifying potential abusers and highlighting those who are careless with paperwork. The audit may reveal areas where costs can be reduced
and have the effect of keeping most employees honest.

What to Look For

There are many cases involving abuse of travel and entertainment expenses. We will relate a few stories that illustrate the
different types of problems to be aware of.

A sales manager claimed that the strand of freshwater pearls

Reducing Employee Transportation Costs

Employee transportation can be a significant cost for many businesses. More than one company that we have examined has found it can reduce its transportation costs without impacting performance in the least.

Reimbursing Employees for Use of Personal Vehicles

Sometimes reimbursing employees for the use of their personal automobiles for company business may have the unwanted result of increasing the amount of travel. This is because a fee based on the IRS allowance per mile is usually more than the out-of-pocket cost of operating the vehicle.* Although the fee is called a reimbursement, in some cases it should be called a subsidy. Reimbursement at the "official" rate may have the unwanted side effect of creating an incentive for the use of personal vehicles and cause the employee to overlook lower cost alternatives.

An employee at a distribution company who was promoted from the warehouse to a desk job accepted the new position without the usual zeal of a man receiving a promotion. We met with him to discover the cause of his hesitation and found he was pleased with the new job but disappointed to learn that he would no longer be required to make a weekly trip to a supplier. The trip was approximately 200 miles, and for three years he had been reimbursed $50 by the company for each weekly trip. (A few months later, at the local pub, the employee was asked why he was so upset about not being able to drive to the supplier. He said that his car was a gas miser and used only $10 worth of fuel for the weekly trip. The extra $160 a month that he received was used for the monthly loan payment on the car.) Since his replacement in the warehouse didn't own a car, the company had reverted to using United Parcel Service for the

---

*The IRS mileage allowance for 1992 was 28¢ per mile. Using this allowance, an "average" automobile that was driven 12,000 miles during the year was eligible to receive up to $3,360.

pickup. The weekly cost to the company was reduced to $14 including insurance. The savings benefit to the company was four additional hours of employee productivity and $36 per week of expenses. Afterwards, no one at the company could say why UPS hadn't been used for the past few years.

What about Company Vehicles?

Many company vehicles are actually luxuries and employee benefits and not necessary for the business. A troubled business must eliminate all vehicles not essential to the business, and if the vehicle is owned by the company, then sell it.

Selling Company-Owned Vehicles

Since at some future date the company may be audited regarding its disposal of company assets, we recommend that you take company-owned vehicles to a local dealer and ask for a written estimate of the value of the vehicles. Alternatively, purchase a copy of the National Association of Auto Dealers (NADA) Blue (retail) or Yellow (wholesale) books of suggested used car values. Use one of these values as a suggested price for selling each vehicle.

Prior to a 1992 precedent-setting case,[1] the retail value of a car would have been the proper valuation of the vehicle. But in the 1992 case, the U.S. Court of Appeals for the Ninth Circuit held that a car need not be valued at its full retail value. Based on this precedent, a company-owned vehicle need not be sold for its NADA retail value, but it should not be sold for less than its NADA wholesale value.

Several times we have observed employees purchasing cars from the company with an arrangement for payments to be made over time through payroll deduction. The problem with this seemingly harmless scenario occurs when the employee later leaves the employ of the company or is laid off. The employee may make countless promises to send weekly checks for the car payments. However, if she has moved out of state, she may never be heard from again. Even with a title to the car, the company's legal recourse may not be worth the cost of recovery. Without the title, the company has no hope of recovery.

The troubled company cannot finance automobile purchases, and there are many institutions that are already in this business. However, if the company is compelled to agree to payments over time, act like a bank and *do not transfer title for the vehicle to the employee until 100 percent of the payments have been made.*

Selling or Exchanging Leased Vehicles

If a company vehicle is leased, discuss terminating the lease with the leasing company or perhaps trading the car in for a less expensive vehicle. Although the cancellation payments on many leases make breaking the lease prohibitive, the dealer may take a Mercedes 300 in trade for two new leases on Chevrolets and will smooth over any rough edges with the leasing company. The company may discover that prepaying several months of lease payments to terminate a lease can be less expensive than continuing for the term. (See the section on leases in Chapter 5 for additional help in this area.)

Lease costs are only one part of the total costs of operating a vehicle. In considering the cost savings of early lease terminations, don't forget to include the costs of operating a vehicle: insurance, fuel, maintenance, and repairs. Particularly in luxury cars, these costs may be significant.

Reducing Wear on Company Vehicles

Another method for reducing costs is to require that employees leave company vehicles at the office on evenings and weekends unless required for work. Wear and tear, mileage, and maintenance can be reduced, and your automobile insurance carrier may reduce your premiums as a result.

Reducing Vehicle Insurance Costs

Insurance for company-owned vehicles can be very expensive. These policies should be reviewed at least annually to determine if costs can be reduced. Don't underinsure, but do examine your policy costs and coverage closely. Here are some suggestions:

- Eliminate coverage for rented automobiles where the company credit card (American Express, etc.) provides coverage at no additional cost.
- Reduce the maximum limit of coverage where the company has a general umbrella policy for catastrophic liability.
- Increase the deductible for collisions or eliminate the coverage.
- Review the list of employees insured and authorized to drive company vehicles. Reduce the list to include only those with good driving records who need to use the vehicles for business.

Reducing General Insurance Costs

A company should examine all of its insurance coverage (property and casualty, liability, workers compensation, business interruption, travel, etc.) and costs at least every two years. Look closely at the business, at the insurance the company needs, and at the coverage the company can realistically afford.

Ask your insurance broker how the company can reduce costs and request competitive bids from other agents. Insurance agents collect a commission for each dollar of premium paid; therefore, there is an economic disincentive to recommend a lower-cost policy when the customer appears satisfied.

Your broker's apparent complacency doesn't mean he needs to be replaced, but always remember: Let the buyer beware. Shop around and make certain that the company has the proper insurance coverage and is getting the best coverage for its premium dollars.

Obtaining Copies of All Insurance Policies

Be certain the company has copies of every insurance policy it is paying premiums for. Insurance agents are not always as diligent as they should be in sending updated or revised policies, and even when they do, you can easily mislay these rarely used documents.

Include in the list of policies any insurance coverage the company has by virtue of its membership in a trade or industry association or corporate credit card program (American Express, Diners Club, etc.). Don't forget to include shipping insurance (Federal Express, United Parcel Service, etc.). Automobile clubs (AAA, Allstate, etc.) traditionally have included coverage for their members for such things as vehicle breakdowns, towing, bail bonds, and trip interruption.

Considering Maintenance Contracts and Warranties

Maintenance contracts are similar to insurance policies in that some have provisions for the loss replacement of equipment that are triggered under specific conditions. Equipment that is usually covered by maintenance contracts includes computers, forklifts, telephone systems, facsimile machines, cellular telephones, pagers, copiers, postage machines, HVAC systems, burglar alarms and security systems, televisions, VCRs, and machine tools.

Included with most new equipment and some used equipment are manufacturer or dealer warranties that may include de facto insurance coverage for repairs, premature breakdown, or fatigue. These types of "insurance" policies may also be included with roof repair or replacement, aluminum siding replacement, insect or pest extermination, landscaping, driveway paving, painting, carpet installation, insulation, basement waterproofing, or fence installation.

Reducing Telecommunications Costs

Most companies do not regularly audit their telephone bills. Audits can be useful by revealing: problems in employee usage of the telephones, fraud committed by nonemployees using the telephone lines (called toll fraud), and areas where costs can be contained or reduced.

Although it can be a mammoth task to audit the bills even for a small company, there are easy ways to achieve the desired results. The following methodology obtains results similar to those of a detailed audit without the need to hire extra staff for the accounting department.

To begin, make auditing the responsibility of each manager. Request that managers explain to each of their employees the high cost of the personal use of business telephones and that no one will be punished, but the practice must stop. Explain to the managers that each department will be expected to review its monthly telecommunications bills and highlight any personal usage. Tell them the company expects payment from any employee who has more than $5 of personal calls in a month. Schedule a meeting in two weeks where the managers are to appear with the marked invoices.

Although the collection of monies owed may not be completely successful, don't be too concerned. The exercise is not intended as a punishment for past sins or as a witch-hunt for any one employee. The objective of the exercise is to instill responsibility and *accountability* for telephone costs at all levels of the company. If the exercise is performed with the proper attitude, it will reduce the company's future telephone bills.

Tell managers the company is also concerned about the excessive use of directory assistance which, at 30¢ to 75¢ per call, can result in unnecessary charges of several dollars per employee per month. Where significant use of directory assistance is found, call the telephone company and ask that a few telephone directories be delivered. Then at the next staff meeting give them to the manager whose employees regularly abuse the directory assistance service. The results will be very effective.

The following month, perform the same exercise. After three months the telephone bills will have decreased an average of 25 percent and the monthly responsibility can be assigned to the accounting department.

Four Easy Steps to Reduce Telephone Costs

1. Inform employees the company will be auditing telephone bills.

2. Request that managers audit their departmental telephone bills.
3. Review the results of the audits at a monthly meeting.
4. Repeat steps 1, 2, and 3 once a month for three months.

The same techniques are very effective in controlling and reducing the costs of cellular telephones and company telephone charge cards.

Watch Out for Area Code 900 Calls and Other Toll Calls

The company should also examine the telephone bills for toll usage for 900-type numbers. When these numbers are called, the charges can range from 25¢ to $25 per minute.

The best example we can remember of 900-number abuse involved the former treasurer of a now defunct savings and loan. Each day the treasurer telephoned the toll numbers for his recorded horoscope (at $5 per minute) and the recorded daily lotto numbers (at $2 per minute) for both New York and neighboring states. In the middle of a meeting, six months before the regulators assumed control of the institution, the treasurer's secretary interrupted and carried into the conference room a packet of blank lotto tickets. The treasurer stopped the meeting and called the 900 number for the previous day's results and then filled out ten new lotto tickets. Without comment, the chief financial officer of a severely distressed $2-billion thrift then continued the meeting!

Other examples include the salesperson who had a girlfriend in another state and called a 900 national weather service (at $3 per minute) to listen to the recorded weather report in her city every day before calling her. (Both calls were at company expense.) Or the sports addict parts manager who dialed a sports number for scores several times a day (at $3 to $5 per minute).

Here are two suggestions to eliminate expenses for 900-type calls:

1. The company's private branch exchange (PBX) may have the option of restricting outgoing 900 calls, or your local

telephone company can block them at the central office. Work with your local and interconnect telephone company to prohibit the connection of 900-type calls.

2. Post a notice to all employees that any 900 calls made will be debited from employees' salary checks and that continued usage of these services from company telephones will be cause for dismissal.

Controlling Company Telephone Charge Cards

Audit and control of telephone charge cards is very poor for many companies. How many telephone charge cards have been issued in your company? Do you have a complete list of the names of all card holders and corresponding account numbers?

In several businesses we found telephone charge cards were issued and *renewed* for former employees who had not worked for the company for over a year. Try recovering damages from an employee who used the card to charge $500 to $1,000 of personal telephone calls and now lives in another state!

Don't perform a witch-hunt. Usually no one person is to blame for the past sins of management. Your objective is to reduce future costs and to instill responsibility and *accountability* for containing and reducing costs at each level of the company.

Obtain a list of all present and former employees who were issued telephone charge cards. Verify this list with the telephone service providers. Request that charge privileges be terminated immediately for anyone who is no longer an employee. Then investigate any usage by former employees and attempt basic collection methods.

Another strategy is to inform employees that all telephone charge cards will be terminated at the end of the month and new cards will be issued. Then request in writing that all telephone service providers terminate all current charge cards. Issue new cards and have them distributed by the personnel department along with a written statement of the policy for using the cards. These terms should include employees' agreement: not to use the card for personal calls, to reimburse the company for any personal calls (if they are made), and not to use the account after the termination of their employment with the company.

Each employee should sign acceptance of the terms and conditions before being given the card.

Limiting the Use of Cellular Telephones

Unless forced at gunpoint, never ever let anyone convince you to provide cellular telephones except to employees who *absolutely and positively* require them for business. Suggest that employees purchase the telephones themselves (even offer to share the cost of the unit), and agree to reimburse them for the monthly activation charges and for any calls made on company business. Cellular telephones can rapidly cost a company hundreds and even thousands of dollars per telephone, per month. For instance, Hydro-Environmental Technologies, a Massachusetts sales and service company, installed car phones for all sales and field personnel. Eight months later, when individual bills were averaging $1,000 per month, the company reduced costs by replacing the cellular telephones with beepers. (A survey commissioned by *Inc.* on the cellular telephone usage of 275 small to midsize companies that issued car phones to their employees concluded that almost one-fourth of the companies felt that the company-provided telephones encouraged abuse, and many companies reported problems until controls such as expense ceilings were implemented.[2])

Request that the cellular service provide a detailed summary of the monthly bill, and use the same technique detailed in the section of this chapter on personal telephone usage. Ask employees to audit their own bills with copies reviewed by their managers.

Auditing Facsimile Machines

The invoices for the telephone lines used for facsimile machines are rarely audited. Don't depend on the audit trail of the fax machine, as it can easily be erased or bypassed. One month, audit the telephone bills for the fax machines and observe any irregularities. It may be harder to find abuses with fax machines but at least if employees know that the company is looking at the bills, then the fear of detection may serve as a deterrent.

We know of one company where an employee regularly faxed the crossword puzzle from *The New York Times* to her father in Europe. When asked if it wasn't expensive, she said, "Probably only $5 per call, but no one looks at the bill anyway."

Auditing Computer and Data Lines

Computer rooms and data communications lines can escape the watchful eye of even the best of auditors. More than once we have found active telephone lines installed for data communications applications being used for personal calls by otherwise honest and hardworking data processing employees. In two cases, the telephone lines had remained active and were used by employees for personal calls for years after the company's requirement for the data lines no longer existed.

During the audit of the telecommunications costs, trace all voice, data, and leased lines (circuits) that the company pays for. Verify all points of origin and destinations for the lines, and confirm that circuits are being used for their intended purpose.

Using Your Vendors' 800 Lines to Reduce Costs

One easy technique for reducing telecommunications costs is to make use of the toll-free lines provided by vendors. These numbers usually have 800 area codes or are leased "tie lines" (also called enterprise lines) that provide a long-distance connection for the price of a local call.

Tie lines are commonly used by banks and financial institutions. This is the approach used by a major New York City bank that uses Manhattan telephone numbers that automatically connect the caller, for the price of a local call, to the bank's customer service department located in another area code sixty miles outside the city.

Ask the managers of each department to list the names of companies commonly telephoned by their subordinates and to research if any provide toll-free numbers. You will be surprised how many numbers your staff regularly call that have toll-free numbers. Call AT&T and ask for a copy of its 800 directory that lists all toll-free numbers issued by AT&T.

Included in the list of companies with toll-free or local numbers are banks, insurance companies, airlines, hotels, car rental agencies, shipping companies, and many customer service lines. Why should your company pay for message units to wait twenty minutes on the line for an airline reservation when using the airline's toll-free number costs the caller nothing?

Also, if your company uses fax or modem data access to its vendors, don't forget that some vendors provide toll-free fax and modem numbers.

Compile a companywide list of all commonly called contacts and their toll-free numbers. Distribute this list to all employees with a note encouraging them to use the toll-free numbers to reduce the company's telecommunications costs.

Using Fax Machines to Reduce Costs

Facsimile communication is a tool that can be used to communicate effectively and expeditiously with less ambiguity and at a lower cost than a voice telephone call. The average one-page letter sent by fax takes less than one minute to transmit. A long-distance voice telephone call to transmit the same information will take more time and therefore be more expensive.

Installing Your Own 800 Line to Reduce Costs

An East Coast domestic manufacturer had several hundred salespersons operating all over the United States, Canada, the Caribbean, and Europe. All of the salespersons telephoned the office several times each week and faxed sales orders. In analyzing telecommunications costs, the company discovered it was paying for the salespersons' calls in one of three ways: reimbursing the salesperson for out-of-pocket costs, paying for the charges on the company-provided telephone charge card, or paying for collect calls to the office.

At the recommendation of its long-distance provider, the company installed a group of incoming 800 circuits that were toll-free to the caller and would be billed directly at a bulk rate to the company. The salespersons were issued a list of the toll-free numbers. Expenses could now be directly controlled from the home office, and the cost of the average telephone call was reduced by 50 percent. The implementation of its own 800-number program reduced costs and was so successful that within a few months the company installed a toll-free circuit for inbound facsimile communications to receive sales orders from the field.

Eliminating Answering Services

Many companies use answering services to receive calls when the receptionist is away from the telephone or the office is closed. For some companies the service is a question of image; for others, it is a necessity to allow emergency callers to reach them. These services can be eliminated by installing answering machines with resulting savings of $50 to $150 per month. Businesses that require emergency callers to reach them can include in the outgoing message a pager number for customers to call in case of an emergency.

Using Pagers

Pagers have become the most inexpensive and reliable method of maintaining contact while out of the office. These devices are significantly less expensive to use than cellular telephones and more reliable. With acquisition costs of $75 to $300 and monthly service fees of $5 to $50, pagers are an inexpensive method for replacing answering services and cellular telephones.

Notes

1. GMAC v. Mitchell, 954 F.2d 557 (9th Cir. 1992).
2. "Car-Phone Pros and Cons," *Inc.*, June 1993, p. 49.

5

Managing Payables

Taming Your Creditors

Getting a handle on accounts payable problems can be difficult when the company is past due with most of its vendors and being harassed by telephone callers asking for payment. The daily calls can interfere with your business and have a demoralizing effect upon the employees who receive the calls.

The solution is to designate one or two persons in your company to receive all telephone calls from creditors. This simple approach limits the interference and effect on morale.

One troubled company was significantly behind in paying its vendors. The accounting department and the receptionist were being bombarded by daily telephone calls from angry vendors. The vendors left lengthy messages detailing the invoice numbers, dates of purchases, and the amounts past due, and they threatened legal action or even worse! For the receptionist the calls were time-consuming and interfered with his ability to answer other calls properly. And, knowing that no funds were available to pay vendors, all the accounting department could do was record the details of the call and verify the dates and amounts of past due invoices.

We recommended the following approach to handle the irate vendors: The assistant controller was designated the contact person for all overdue accounts payable. A new telephone line bypassing the switchboard with direct incoming access from the outside was installed into her office. The telephone had an answering machine attached that gave a pleasant greeting inviting callers to leave a brief message and advising them that the assistant controller would be in the office on Monday, Wednesday, and Friday afternoons and would respond to *all* messages received only on those days.

The angry vendors required approximately two weeks to tame. Initially, vendors still attempted to reach the switchboard or the accounting department, but the receptionist always transferred the calls to the new accounts payable extension, where the caller heard the recording from the assistant controller's new answering machine.

On the designated afternoons, the assistant controller dutifully returned all telephone calls received. Although there was usually no substantive news to report to the vendors, they appreciated having their calls returned. The other people in the company were now free to perform their jobs unimpaired.

Once you have tamed the problem of vendor harassment, the next step is to verify and correctly value the current accounts.

Verifying Accounts Payable

Listings of accounts payable (A/P) are usually fraught with errors. Before you can begin to make choices as to whom to pay and how much to pay, you need to have an accurate listing.

Errors creep into the A/P listing in a number of ways. Common causes are: paying the same invoice twice, payments made but not recorded by the vendor, payments made but not recorded by your company, partial shipments being paid in full, returns to vendors not being recorded as credits, and errors in invoices received from vendors being left unchecked and entered into the A/P system. (The company should never pay for products or services that were delivered damaged, failed to perform, or were not usable. Many computerized A/P systems do not include the provision for placing a hold on paying an invoice because of problems with the merchandise or services.)

Discovering later that the company overpaid a vendor during a month it was unable to meet payroll is a painful lesson to learn. When managing a company with insufficient cash flow, verifying the A/P ensures that the company pays only those invoices it owes.

If the task of verifying each invoice is too tedious, then at the least try to verify all invoices that are greater than $100.

To verify accounts payable, first generate a *complete* list of the A/P. (This list is also one of the required items when filing for bankruptcy, so keeping it accurate and current is useful contingency planning.) In doing so:

- Include for each vendor the contact name, telephone and fax numbers, details for each unpaid invoice, aging information for each unpaid invoice, and details on any returned products or requests for credit.
- Ask managers if there were any problems with any of the invoices, i.e., faulty products, partial shipments, back-ordered parts, incomplete or less than satisfactory service, or products that lacked merchantability.
- Spot-check the invoices against the company's purchase orders, shipping records, and warehouse receipts.
- Audit where problems are uncovered with the spot checks.
- Request credit (in writing) from the vendor for any problems discovered, and obtain verification of the credit memorandum (in writing) from the vendor.

The next step is to call each vendor:

- Verify each invoice in the list of payables.
- Ask the vendor (in writing) to send copies of any missing invoices.
- Verify each payment made by the company during the last six months.
- If the investigation reveals any discrepancies, then request (in writing) that the vendor produce copies of each invoice (and proof of delivery, if required) for the past six months.

During the telephone verification of the A/P, be careful not to commit to a payment schedule with any vendors. Let them know, without question, that the purpose of the inquiry is to verify the outstanding invoices, not to make promises about the future disbursement of funds. Without being too specific, tell vendors that the company is "restructuring" its finances and should be contacting them within two weeks to discuss outstanding invoices.

With an accurate list of payables, you can make decisions on which vendors to schedule for payments, when, and for how much.

Don't Worry: You Can Negotiate

Don't assume that because you now have an accurate A/P listing with a total of $650,000 owed to vendors, $500,000 of which is past due, that the amount that the company will ultimately be required to pay vendors will be $650,000. A troubled business can use its misfortune to gain added flexibility from vendors when negotiating payments and terms for amounts past due. You may ultimately be required to pay less than the total amount owed to vendors.

Negotiating with Vendors

When a company is having problems meeting payroll and paying its monthly rent, owing $350,000 to a vendor that is sixty to ninety days overdue may seem like an insurmountable problem. Don't worry—most vendors are reasonable businesspersons.

Think about how much your company and your vendors have in common. Vendors want to be paid at least something. They want to keep your company as a customer, and you can use this to your advantage when negotiating. Show them respect and talk to them. Vendors do not want to litigate to collect debts because: (1) they might not win in court, (2) they would lose you as a customer, and (3) litigation is a very lengthy process. But neither do vendors want to forgive and forget the entire amount you owe them.

Your company would like to pay the vendor as little as possible and to make these payments over an extended period of time. Your company does not want to suffer the harassment of

Exhibit 5-1. Points to remember when negotiating with vendors.

What Vendors Want	What Vendors Don't Want
• To be paid something	• To write off 100 percent of the debt
• To be treated with respect	• To be ignored
• To have payments = respect	• To wait forever to be paid
• To avoid litigation	• To litigate
• To keep you as a customer	• To lose a future customer
What You Want	*What You Don't Want*
• To pay as little as possible	• To pay 100 percent of the debt today
• To make payments over an extended period	• To be harassed by angry creditors
• To maintain vendor relationships	• To have unrealistic payment schedules
• To avoid litigation	• To litigate

an angry creditor or lose a relationship with a vendor that has taken several years to build. The common ground that exists between your company and your vendors is a big advantage in negotiating. See Exhibit 5-1 for points to remember when negotiating with vendors.

Your company does not have the funds to pay all creditors on a current basis, so you need to examine each creditor on an individual basis and choose a plan of action based on each one's position and your present and future needs for the creditor.

Categorizing Your Creditors

Divide creditors into four categories. The first category (vital payments), the highest priority, is limited to payments required on a regularly scheduled basis for the business to continue. Extended payment terms might still be negotiated, but your flexibility is limited. Vital payments can include: current payroll, insurance, utilities, taxes, professional fees, and sometimes rents and lease payments. The remaining three categories of creditors—A, B, and C—are based on the company's present and future needs for each vendor's goods or services. (See Exhibit 5-2.)

Exhibit 5-2. Vendor categories.

1. *Vital payments:*	Current payroll, insurance, utilities, taxes, professional fees, and some rents and lease payments
2. *A-list vendors:*	Sole source suppliers
3. *B-list vendors:*	Multiple source suppliers
4. *C-list vendors:*	No longer necessary

If a vendor provided asphalt for the driveway and the company is unlikely to need additional asphalt in the next twelve months, then the vendor receives a low priority for receiving any payments. (Care should be taken to avoid assigning a low priority to vendors who are in a position to assert a lien on the company's property for nonpayment of an invoice.) The United Parcel Service and the telephone company, on the other hand, are vendors the company needs on a daily basis and for which there are usually no alternative suppliers. Both would receive a high ranking in the priority of vendors to be paid.

Rank all vendors according to the company's future need to continue doing business with them. The A list are high priority suppliers. These vendors provide products or services that the business depends on, and typically they are the sole sources for these goods. For example, if the company is primarily a dealer of RCA televisions, this list includes RCA.

The B list includes suppliers who provide goods that the company requires for the business but that can be purchased from other sources. For a car dealership, this list would include tire manufacturers and petroleum product distributors, of which there are several alternative suppliers.

The C list includes suppliers who are not unique in their pricing or in the services they deliver or whom the company will not be needing in the next year. Examples are a janitorial service, an office supply dealer, or a roof repair service. All of these suppliers can be replaced by another vendor with similar pricing.

Vendors on the A list deserve the most attention. You need to concentrate your efforts on negotiating with these vendors a payment schedule that both the company and the vendors can live with.

Vendors on the B list include many that can be negotiated with. The company has leverage over B vendors because it may not require them in the future since there are alternatives. If B vendors are willing to work with the company through the troubled times, then they may receive some payments soon. But B vendors who won't work with the company quickly become a member of the C list. Vendors on the C list are unlikely to receive any payment until the company has stabilized its financial condition.

Analyzing Each Vendor's Negotiating Position

When analyzing each vendor and planning the approach to negotiate monies owed, consider the following factors: the vendor's willingness to work with the company during this troubled period, his size and sophistication, the amount the company owes him, the influence he has, and indirectly, the priority (for receiving payment) the vendor would receive in a bankruptcy filing or insolvency proceeding.

- *Willingness to work with you.* Business is business, but a vendor's willingness to be understanding and flexible during a troubled period can be very valuable to the cash-starved company. A vendor who is owed payment on long overdue invoices and agrees to continue to make small shipments of critical goods necessary to maintain your business has shown a willingness to work with you during a troubled period and may deserve some favoritism in being paid.

- *Size and sophistication.* A vendor with total accounts receivable of $200 million may be less concerned with the company's debt of $200,000 than a small local vendor who is owed $900. This is particularly true if the vendor needs the $900 to pay her own rent. By "concerned" we mean: the vendor's patience before litigating, her willingness to forgive a portion of the debt, and her willingness to negotiate an extended payment schedule.

Large and sophisticated creditors are more willing to negotiate a reduction in the total amount owed. Despite their protests that they have "never done this before," they are usually very experienced at negotiating these types of adjustments. They know the pitfalls of litigation and although they are the first to threaten, they wait the longest before initiating legal action.

Smaller and unsophisticated creditors are less likely to negotiate and may argue that even a 10 percent reduction in the amount owed would be unfair to them and unacceptable.

• *Amount the company owes.* Most small vendors will not begin to litigate for amounts less than $1,000, and most larger creditors will not litigate for amounts less than $10,000, but be aware that there are exceptions to this rule.

Try to estimate the amount of leverage that the company has over the vendor. The maxim that was repeated frequently at the time of Donald Trump's recent troubles and during the continuing saga of the Olympia & York bankruptcies was that if you owe a bank $1 million you have a big problem, but if you owe a bank $100 million, then *the bank* has a problem! We would add another level: If you owe the bank $10 million, then both of you have a problem.

During a difficult period for your industry, even a relatively small debt of $25,000 to $50,000 can be very significant to a vendor. The more significant the debt is to a vendor, the more leverage you should have in negotiating. The objective of negotiations is to achieve a reduction in the total amount owed and extended payment terms in exchange for a promise of regular payments.

The company may also have leverage with a vendor by its market position. Your company's strategic importance to the vendor translates to leverage when negotiating. For example, if your company is a manufacturer's only Florida distributor, then you are of strategic importance to the manufacturer until it finds a replacement. This value is your leverage when negotiating. It may be less expensive for the manufacturer to be flexible and to work with you during the troubled period than to recruit and build a relationship with a new distributor.

• *Influence the vendor has.* A vendor whose president is also on the board of the bank that holds a loan you have defaulted on, or a vendor who is influential with other members of your industry, may warrant special treatment.

• *Priority the vendor would have in bankruptcy.* Although you may not be planning to file for bankruptcy in the near future, a troubled company should always be cognizant of a creditor's potential standing in a bankruptcy court. Is the creditor's claim secured or unsecured? Would she have a priority to receive payment under the Bankruptcy Code? See Chapter 11 of this book on bankruptcy for a full description of these priorities.

There are two reasons why it is important to know a creditor's potential priority in bankruptcy: (1) if the situation worsens the creditor may try to force you into an involuntary bankruptcy, and (2) if you are ever in bankruptcy you want to know the effect of having paid the creditor today.

Creditors who could force you into bankruptcy deserve special attention not to be angered, and you may opt to withhold payment for those who would be a priority in bankruptcy.

How to Negotiate with Vendors

The objective when negotiating with vendors is to gain and retain as much flexibility as possible. Stay in telephone contact with your vendors and let them know who is managing the relationship. Don't let them be the leader. If they start calling every day, tell them clearly and firmly that you will speak to them, say, every Thursday. Vendors are rarely incorrigible and are usually easy to tame. (Remember the example of the A/P manager who put a message on her answering machine that she would be in Disneyland for a week and received no complaints when she returned.)

Before contacting each vendor, review your negotiating position. (See Exhibit 5-3.) Write down those elements of your company's relationship with the vendor that give you additional leverage. Remember the common interests that you share with the vendors. Use both the company's leverage and any common ground as tools for negotiating.

Don't reveal to the creditor your entire tool belt in the first

Exhibit 5-3. Prioritization of accounts payable.

Description of Payment	Payment Priority			
	Vital	A	B	C
Payroll and commissions				
Current	Yes			
Past due				✔
Pension funding				✔
Trust fund taxes				
Withholding	Yes			
FICA	Yes			
Sales tax	Yes			
Corporate taxes				
Federal	Negotiate	✔		
State	Negotiate	✔		
Local	Negotiate	✔		
Secured creditors				
Mortgages	Negotiate	✔	✔	
Loans	Negotiate	✔	✔	
Leasing companies				
Vehicles	Negotiate	✔	✔	
Equipment	Negotiate	✔	✔	
Unsecured creditors				
Rent	Negotiate	✔	✔	✔
Insurance	Negotiate	✔		
Utilities	Negotiate	✔		
Professional fees	Negotiate	✔		
Travel and entertainment		✔	✔	✔
Freight, FEDEX, UPS, etc.	Negotiate	✔	✔	
Vendors				
A-list vendors		✔		
B-list vendors			✔	
C-list vendors				✔

telephone conversation. Generally, you would like to stretch the negotiating process out over several weeks. The more time that elapses while you are in the negotiation phase, the more time you or others in your company have to effect a recovery of the business before having to pay any part of the debt.

Handling Litigation

The troubled company should avoid litigation where possible and always *appear* to be concerned about the threat of creditor lawsuits. However, never forget that regarding leverage in negotiating, when the creditor stops talking and initiates litigation he has lost. Assuming that you have only flimsy defenses for nonpayment, the *absolute minimum* time required in most states from the initiation of a suit to the creditor receiving a judgment is six to twelve months! And don't forget: There is also a possibility that the creditor will get her day in court and lose her case or receive only a partial judgment.

During the time that a creditor's lawsuit is winding its way through the legal labyrinth, your company will be growing financially stronger, and the creditor will be spending money to prove her case while still waiting to be paid.

You don't need to educate the company's vendors to the pitfalls of litigation, but if they go over the edge, then try the following approach: Tell the creditor his choice is unfortunate, the outcome in court is not a certain judgment, and that with some additional patience he might do better standing by you during these troubled times. Ask the creditor to consider your offer and agree to telephone him in a week. Most creditors will bluff several times before initiating litigation; it's your job not to let them fall out of the ring. Always leave creditors room to return to the negotiating arena. You can play hardball later.

Negotiating with Different Categories of Vendors

Vital Payments

As stated earlier, these are payments that absolutely and positively (with apologies to Federal Express) must be paid regularly, in full, for the company to remain in business. From time to time vendors categorized as vital can be convinced to accept payments under terms and conditions similar to those on the A list. However, unlike A vendors, the terms granted by vital vendors are usually a onetime forbearance, for one week or one month.

You have some flexibility with vital payments, but not much. You can usually negotiate the following types of arrangements: spreading (or financing) of annual insurance premiums into quarterly or monthly payments, spreading a monthly rental into weekly payments, or deferring payment of a large commission check into several partial payments.

A-List Vendors

The objective in negotiating with vendors on the A list is to agree mutually to write off a portion of the debt in conjunction with an agreement to stay current with all new invoices and to make payments on the balance due over an extended period. Paying $150,000 at one time may be too much for you, but negotiating to be forgiven for $70,000 of the debt and to pay the balance of $80,000 in ten monthly installments may be manageable and acceptable. (Your leverage is that they want to be paid something.)

Use your leverage that they are willing to accept a reduction in the debt and have a vested interest in your remaining in business. Tell each vendor that as much as you would like to pay all of your debts, doing so would put you out of business, which wouldn't benefit either of your companies. Wouldn't a fresh start, where you would agree to remain current on all future invoices, benefit both of you (using common interests and the leverage that the vendor wants to keep you as a customer)?

B-List Vendors

Vendors on the B list are those whom you can replace, though not necessarily without some external costs. If vendors show a willingness to work with your company during its troubled period and continue to do business with you, then they deserve your respect. Try to allocate some funds to make token payments to these vendors. Even nominal payments are received favorably because they show your respect (remember: payments = respect) for the vendor.

When making payments to B vendors, always send them to the attention of a particular individual. The company may have a lockbox or a post office box for accepting payments, but don't use it. Your purpose in making a payment is more to show your respect than to make a significant dent in the total debt owed the vendor. (Another reason for sending payments to an individual's attention instead of a lockbox is the extra one to two days of float before the check is deposited and clears the bank.)

Make the payment a personal gesture between two businesspersons. Telephone the recipient and inform *him* you are sending a payment. It's a small payment, but you want *him* to know you are making a strong effort under difficult circumstances.

If the B vendor cannot be persuaded to agree to terms acceptable to the company's current financial position and refuses to continue doing business with you, then relegate him to the C list. Continue negotiating, but pay him nothing!

C-List Vendors

The only purpose in negotiating with vendors that you have relegated to this category is to avoid the nuisance and cost to your company of defending multiple small lawsuits. You may eventually be in a position to pay some of these vendors, but not today and not for the next few months.

"Nice guys finish last."*

As much as you may be sympathetic to the plight of vendors relegated to the C list, never forget that your company is fighting to stay alive.

In the recovery mode you cannot afford to do any favors (i.e., make any payments) to vendors unless you need the vendor's cooperation to survive.

*Leo Durocher, baseball manager and player (1906–1991)

Any "favors" that you grant this month may come at
the expense of your own paycheck next month!

Leases

Leases can be grouped into three basic categories based on the
type of asset being leased: vehicle, equipment, or real estate.
Also of importance is whether the lease is an obligation of the
corporation or if an officer or employee cosigned (guaranteed or
accepted joint responsibility) for the obligation.

If an individual accepted *joint responsibility* for the lease,
then the lessor would have the right to recover from both the
company and the individual in the event of a default or for any
damages sustained by early termination of the lease. If an individual *guaranteed* the lease, then the lessor could recover damages from the individual *only* after the lessor had failed in its
attempts to collect from the company. Some leases have provisions that bring the guaranty into force immediately upon a default of certain terms of the lease. See Chapter 8 for a detailed
treatment of lease issues.

*Ask your company's attorney to review each of the leases and to
identify the responsible parties and the order and trigger conditions for
each obligation.* Analysis of obligations and guaranties relating to
leases is also necessary to understand the effects of a potential
bankruptcy filing or insolvency proceeding.

Vehicle Leases

Why are lenders holding vehicle leases difficult to negotiate with
and reluctant even to begin negotiations? The reasons for their
position are simple: Why should they negotiate? They have good
security and usually have additional recourse against individuals
in the company.

The security for the lease, the vehicle, has a ready market;
therefore, the lessor could take possession of the vehicle and
either sell or lease it again. Any damage to the vehicle (the lessor's security) is covered by required insurance. Most vehicle
leases for small and medium-size businesses require that an of-

ficer cosign or guaranty the obligation. This means that if the company defaults on the lease, the lessor would have legal remedies against others.

Therefore, given the lessor has reliable security and more than one pocket to go after, these lenders are the least likely to negotiate better terms, but there are still ways to tame them:

• If the vehicle has recurrent service problems and the company leased it through a dealer, there may be recourse available under state law (lemon laws) to withhold lease payments until the vehicle is satisfactorily repaired.

• Most dealers conduct their leasing under a separate company or sell the lease to a finance company within a few days or months. The dealer may tell you that its sale of the lease to a finance company located 2,000 miles away relieves it of any obligation. However, the contract under which it sold the lease to the finance company, or the laws in your state, may not support the dealer. Ask legal counsel to review the terms of the company's leases for any options or recourse you may have for vehicles that have not performed as promised.

• Before negotiating with the lessor, decide what the company would like to do with the leased vehicle. The options are: return the vehicle to the lessor, transfer the obligation to another company, transfer the obligation to an individual, exchange the vehicle for alternate transportation, sell the vehicle, pay the lease cancellation fees, or purchase the remainder of the lease. (These will be discussed in detail later.)

• Don't be under the mistaken belief that, because the lease terms say that the lease is not assumable and the company is not free to sell the vehicle, your company is limited in its options. Just because it is written in a contract doesn't mean that a lender won't agree to these types of arrangements. When faced with the prospect of chasing the monthly payments and possibly repossessing the underlying security through the legal system, a lessor may be very willing to accept a new lessee or agree to the sale of the vehicle to a third party.

• Prove to the lessor that a proposed option is to its advantage (this probably won't work). Be forceful. Tell the lessor the choice is to let your company off the hook and accept revenue today from a new source or learn to be very patient waiting for payments. Don't tell the lessor to begin collection procedures; people there know their jobs, and if they don't, it's not to your advantage to educate them. If you are reasonable, but firm, the lessor may exhibit some flexibility.

> *Warning:* If the lessor has agreed to alternate terms and conditions, always confirm the proposed understanding in writing, but never assume any obligations without consulting legal counsel.

Be particularly careful when a lessor releases the company from an obligation. The release must also extend to any individuals or entities with joint responsibility for, or who acted as guarantors for, the company's performance under the lease.

Let's look at your specific options with a leased vehicle.

1. *Returning the vehicle to the lessor.* Try to reach a mutual agreement before returning a vehicle to the lessor. The company does not need to have agreed to all of the terms under which the vehicle is being returned, but the company's position in a legal proceeding may be more defensible if the lessor has agreed to take possession of the vehicle.

We have heard of situations where lessees have returned vehicles by driving the vehicle onto the front lawn of the lessor, locking the car, and leaving with the keys. You may have heard the news story about the man who left the vehicle in the lessor's lobby after crashing through a plate glass window! The lessor had refused to renegotiate the expiration date of the lease. Although these methods may give personal satisfaction, they are not recommended approaches.

> *Warning:* Upon return of the vehicle, the lessor may "discover" damage, excessive wear and tear, or other problems. Before returning the vehicle, to protect the company, take complete and close-up color photographs of the vehicle, both inside and outside, and retain these along with a full copy of all service records.

6

Managing Receivables

Receivables are those funds that would flow into the company's coffers were the business to continue normal operations (i.e., your cash flow). Receivables can include: payments by customers (traditional accounts receivable), refunds from tax authorities, insurance settlements, credits and overcharges from vendors, rents, royalties, lease payments, and proceeds from sales of assets. Each receivable requires a different management and collection strategy. The first distinction is between receivables due from customers and other receivables.

Receivables from Customers

Similar to the approach when taming the payables problem, a priority for a troubled business is to assemble an accurate list of all accounts receivable (A/R). When compiling this list of A/R, it is also prudent to assemble a dossier on each customer. There are two reasons for the dossiers: (1) The company may want to sell the customer list and having a complete dossier will make the sale easier. (2) If the company decides to give problem receivables to a collection agency, the dossiers will increase the likelihood of a recovery.

Pay particular attention to accounts that might have been written off or marked uncollectible during the past twelve

months. Collusion between the company's employees and customers can result in mysterious changes to receivables. Receivables from customers that were written off may also prove
collectible when turned over to a collection agency or an attorney who specializes in collection.

A/R are often marked uncollectible because although the invoice represents goods or services that were delivered to the customer, there was a misunderstanding with the customer and the
salesperson responsible for the account did not want to interfere
with a future business relationship. If the company is terminating the operation, it is unlikely to have a future business relationship with the customer; with no holds barred, a collection
agency or attorney may find the debt collectible in part, if not
in whole.

The A/R can easily contain errors, omissions, and inaccura-
cies. All invoices for the past twelve months should be compared to documents such as purchase orders and shipping
manifests to substantiate their accuracy. Cross-checking the A/R
with other documents may point to potential fraud, and unknown (or hidden) assets can be revealed.

A wholesale distributor terminating an export division discovered many pieces of equipment priced at $5,000 to $25,000
each with a total market value of almost $500,000 not fully ac-
counted for. Each piece of equipment had been shipped to customers as demonstration models or samples over the past three
years without any receivable being generated. No obvious fraud
was revealed, but after invoicing the customers for these "samples," the company received $140,000 of payments and the re-
turn of $190,000 of merchandise. This amounted to a recovery
rate of approximately 66 percent! How much higher would the
recovery rate have been if management had reviewed accounts
receivable every six months?

Collecting Receivables from Customers

The approach that a company needs to take with respect to its
receivables from customers depends on the path that it has chosen for that segment of the business. There are two components:

Exhibit 6-1. Plan for collecting receivables from customers.

Survival Plan	Strategy	Desired Result
Increase revenues	☎ Negotiate	✛ Dovetail
Reduce operations	☎ Negotiate	/ Accelerate
Sell the company	✔ Collect	✄ Discount
Terminate all operations	✔ Collect	✄ Discount

the *strategy* and the *desired result*. Both relate to the company's survival plan. (See Exhibit 6-1.)

Increase Revenues

If the survival plan for the business is to concentrate upon and increase that portion of the operations that the receivables relate to, then use your current receivable as leverage to grow your business.

Inform your present customers of your plans and encourage them (i.e., use your marketing skills on them) to include your group of products and services in their future purchases. *Negotiate* with the customer and *dovetail* any invoices due from her with new invoices for additional goods and services. Consider promotions such as offering customers special discounts for new orders when accompanied by prepayment.

Reduce Operations

When reducing operations to reduce costs or increase profitability, there is a possibility that the result may alter and possibly damage existing relationships with customers and affect your future ability to collect on the receivable. The concern is genuine: When changing the nature of your business, you should not expect your customers to greet your changes with open arms.

Balance your schedule for reducing operations with your progress in negotiations with customers relating to current and past due receivables. Your strategy should be to *negotiate* with the objective of *accelerating* the payments. The benefit is that if the customers react to the company's plans by not withholding or delaying payments, the cash flow will be increased and the amount of receivables at risk will be reduced.

Sell the Company

The status of receivables (i.e., their value) when selling a business is a significant concern to both the buyer and the seller. If the buyer is concerned about the future ability to collect receivables, then he will discount their value. One possible reaction of the seller is to remove the receivables from the sale and to collect as much as possible prior to closing. If the buyer has confidence in the value of the receivables, he may demand that the entire list be included in the purchase. This can present a problem if a customer pays a receivable during the due diligence period (i.e., before closing).

No seller of a troubled business should ever give up cash in hand, and therein lies the dilemma. The only solution is to accept the fact that there will be minor adjustments to the purchase price of a business at the closing.

Your mission in selling a troubled business is to maximize the cash you can legally take from the business prior to the closing. Make every possible effort to *collect* outstanding receivables before the closing date.

Terminate All Operations

Terminating operations can be very hazardous to the health (collection) of your receivables. If you have made the decision to terminate a business, then move quickly to *collect* all of the accounts receivable today. Do not delay and do not inform your customers of your decision to terminate until after you have collected the majority of your receivables.

When selling a business or terminating operations your strategy for collecting receivables is similar: Collect it today. You may not have the ability to collect the monies in the future. Therefore, even if collection today requires taking a substantial *discount*, it may be worth it. The following list summarizes the basic strategies for converting your receivables into cash in the bank.

How to Convert Receivables into Cash

1. Offer the customers *discounts* of 20 percent for early payments.
2. If a customer offers to mail you a check, suggest that you or someone else from the company will *personally* pick it up today. (Don't delay.)
3. For any receivables where a dispute exists with the customer, make an offer of compromise. Split the difference.
4. Don't be greedy. Get the cash!

Other Receivables

Receivables can come from many sources other than your customers. Don't ignore all the other sources. Many a business has terminated operations only to discover six months or a year later that receivables existed they were not aware of. *Examine all avenues for recovering monies due the company.*

Refunds and Credits

- Refunds from tax authorities
- Insurance settlements and overpayments
- Credits, overcharges, and reimbursements from vendors
- Co-op advertising and promotional credits
- Refunds for canceled travel arrangements
- Royalties, rents, and lease payments
- Reimbursements from employees

Deposits

- Security deposits on utilities, real estate, and equipment
- Deposits for mailing fees
- Advance deposits for appearances in trade shows and conferences
- Other deposits

Collecting Other Receivables

Refunds and Credits

• *Refunds from tax authorities.* Just because the company is behind on some tax obligations does not mean that all departments of the federal, state, or local taxing authorities communicate with each other or are even aware of the delinquency. We have observed companies that owe hundreds of thousands of dollars in past due taxes requesting and receiving checks from the government for tens of thousands of dollars of overpayments from prior periods. *If you don't discuss other taxes or periods, taxing authorities may not even look for them.*

To get refunds from taxing authorities:

• Make requests in writing and keep them short and simple.
• Do not mention any periods other than the period during which there was an overpayment or refund due.
• Write a separate letter for each overpayment and request payment by check.
• Do not allow past overpayments to be applied to future taxes.

• *Insurance settlements and overpayments.* If the company is due any settlements for claims, then negotiate and offer to take a small discount in exchange for a speedy disposition. If the company has made estimated insurance payments but the business has decreased, request a refund.

Insurance overpayments are most common with unemployment and workers compensation insurance, where the premium is based on a formula determined by the types of employees, their salaries, and the total payroll. If the company reduced its personnel roster or salaries during the past two years, it should have submitted an updated census of your personnel to the insurance carrier. If the census has not been done, then do it today and include the effective date of every employment termination or salary reduction.

Request in writing, separately from each insurer, a check for each overpayment. Do not permit the overpayment to be applied to a future or past-due premium. The company needs the cash today!

• *Credits, overcharges, and reimbursements from vendors.* Did the company return inventory or product to a vendor, but it has not received proper credit? Did the company make a duplicate payment for an invoice or overpay for goods? Do not delay; ask for payment today. Fax the vendor a letter requesting a check. Don't accept a credit unless you absolutely must. Explain to the vendor that your accounting system cannot handle a credit and you must receive a check to keep your records straight. Try saying it—you never know. If the vendor hasn't read this book, it just might work to get you the money.

Is the company entitled to reimbursements from vendors for performing warranty repairs, special services, or promotions? Be certain all claim forms have been submitted and request an expedited check today. Again, ask for a check, not a credit against payables. Tell the vendor that reimbursements and purchases are handled by separate departments and that the company needs to receive a check to offset the receivable. Try saying it—it just might work.

• *Co-op advertising and promotional credits.* Co-op advertising and promotional credits are "earned" when the company sells products of another company with a formal cooperative or marketing promotions program. Typically these programs reimburse you for advertising and marketing efforts equivalent to 2 or 3 percent of sales of the manufacturer's products.

If the company owes the manufacturer money, it may be required to offset the amount owed by the value in the co-op account. More frequently, these programs are administered by independent service bureaus that administer co-op programs for hundreds of manufacturers, and you can request a check from them without even mentioning any amounts past due the manufacturer. A troubled business may be unaware that it is sitting upon thousands or tens of thousands of dollars of co-op funds.

• *Refunds for canceled travel arrangements.* Particularly if the company is scaling back or terminating operations, it may have canceled travel plans for which it purchased airline tickets, pre-paid hotel arrangements, or booked conventions. Don't delay. Request a check for the cancellation and submit all airline tickets directly for reimbursement.

If the company is not eligible to receive refunds, try to sell the travel arrangements to another company. If these travel arrangements are related to a trade show or conference, advertise the prepaid arrangements in trade publications and you will probably find a buyer.

• *Royalties, rents, and lease payments.* If the company receives royalty or license payments, consider offering a discount for accelerated payments. If the company receives monthly royalties, offer a discount to the licensee prepaying next year's license fees or royalties in advance. If the company receives payments based on production quantities or quantities sold, offer a discount on quantity to the payee making advance payments for the next six or twelve months.

• *Reimbursements from employees.* Check with the company's bookkeeping or human resources department. If current employees owe the company money, immediately start collection procedures. Give the employees ten days to make arrangements for repayment or start deducting from their next paycheck.

If past employees owe the company money, make a strong effort to collect. If the amount is greater than $500, initiate legal action to recover the funds.

Deposits

• *Security deposits on utilities, real estate, and equipment.* Has the company terminated leases or vacated properties during the past three years? If so, did the company receive all of the security deposits due on utilities? *Request these deposits today.*

If the company has terminated telephone services or reduced the number of lines at a facility, it may have an excess amount on deposit as security for payment. Don't worry that the company owes money on other bills to the same utility. Utilities are like taxing authorities when it comes to refunds. They can be litigating to collect monies on one account and issue a refund check on another account even if both accounts have the same service name and address.

• *Deposits for mailing fees.* If the company does frequent mass mailings or uses a business reply mail permit or a postage meter, it is required to deposit sufficient funds to cover several months of expected usage. The company won't receive refunds on these deposits unless you ask for them.

Several times we have been involved in the search for deposits at the post office with profitable results. Joan Cook, once a leader in the mail-order business, filed for bankruptcy in early 1992. Several months later, the chief financial officer remembered a $70,000 deposit with the post office that was recovered for the benefit of creditors. Unfortunately, these funds should have been available to the company prior to terminating operations, not afterward.

• *Advance deposits for appearances in trade shows and conferences.* The company may be entitled to refunds for advance deposits on trade shows and conferences. Or it may be able to sell the registration or display space to another company. Advertise the space in trade publications and you will probably find a buyer.

• *Other deposits.* Many other services require security deposits. Don't ignore these deposits. You won't see them if you don't request them. Included in this list are deposits on vending machines, LP (liquified petroleum) gas containers, garbage and recycling dumpsters, pagers, and cellular telephones.

Looking Everywhere for Assets

Examine all possible avenues for recovering assets when terminating business operations.

With company-owned equipment or other company assets in the personal possession of employees, try to sell the assets to the employees (at fair market value). If the company requests the equipment but it is not returned, don't hesitate to hold back a payroll check due the employee until the property is returned. If an employee is being terminated, he may not feel any obligation to return property. He may even feel a grudge against the company, which, in his own mind, justifies the conversion of company property to his own.

We have seen cars, computers, fax machines, cellular telephones, pagers, VCRs, televisions, paper shredders, hand trucks, tools, software, books, and cameras disappear because of the failure to ask for their return or the failure to request the return at the proper time (i.e., before the last payroll or commission check was issued).

7

Terminating And Reducing Operations

The "Image" Problem

For most entrepreneurs it is easier to start a new business than to terminate or reduce existing operations. The reasons are purely machismo, ego, and self-image. Those who view terminating operations as synonymous with defeat must remember that the primary objective in a rescue mission is to stabilize the company's financial position. It is usually neither profitable nor feasible for the company to maintain all of its current operations while recovering from its troubles.

An unprofitable real estate brokerage may not have enough business to support two office locations, but it could be profitable when paying the overhead of only one location. The closing of the second office is not a defeat. It is a prudent and necessary business decision. Once the decision has been made and the termination completed, the brokerage's deteriorating financial condition will be stabilized and the first objective of its recovery will have been achieved.

When terminating or reducing operations, do not confuse the image of success with the need to return a company to financial health. If the company needs to sell the Mercedes or the airplane to pay the bills, don't hesitate. If the company needs to close its offices and move to less expensive space, do it today and start counting the money saved.

Many entrepreneurs get caught up in "looking successful" instead of managing a company through difficult times to remain profitable. Don't worry about how successful your neighbor or competitor is. Your neighbor may look successful, but don't be surprised if her image of success is a lifestyle beyond her means.*

Although debtors can lead "lifestyles of the rich and famous" without committing illegal acts, two debtors who flamboyantly danced their way into the bankruptcy court and were later convicted on criminal charges relating to their spending habits were Marvin Mitchelson and William R. Runnells, Jr.

Divorce lawyer Marvin Mitchelson made "palimony" a household word by successfully representing the live-in companion of actor Lee Marvin. In Mitchelson's trial for tax evasion following his bankruptcy filing, witnesses testified that even as the public utilities were shutting off his services for nonpayment, Mitchelson continued to spend money on limousines, hotel suites, and antiques.

In the early 1980s, William R. Runnells, Jr., founded and guided Landbank Equity Corporation through its meteoric rise to become one of the largest second-mortgage companies on the East Coast. Landbank filed for bankruptcy in 1987 with liabilities exceeding $100 million. According to news reports, Runnells frequently came to bankruptcy proceedings in a chauffeured Jaguar. Until he was jailed for refusing to answer questions relating to his assets, Runnells continued to live a flamboyant lifestyle. (Runnells was eventually jailed in 1987 by a district judge in

---

*A personal anecdote on the illusory image of success involves two companies, both of which appeared to be very successful: Businessland, Inc. (the computer retailer) and Integrated Resources, Inc. (the investment firm). While managing a small computer company, we proposed to sell a system to Integrated. Several weeks later, a representative from Integrated called and said that although we had the best product, because of concerns about the "future financial viability" of our company Integrated had chosen Businessland. Within a year, history delivered a Pyrrhic victory. Integrated filed for bankruptcy protection and Businessland was insolvent. We then realized that we were more financially stable and viable than either of these two "images of success."

Norfolk, Virginia, on civil contempt charges for failing to disclose the location of assets in a bankruptcy proceeding and continuing to sell assets after filing for bankruptcy.)

The newspapers are full of cases of insolvent entities whose principals drove up in limousines to file for bankruptcy. These individuals may have maintained the image of being successful, but they did not make the decisions necessary to earn enough profit to support their lifestyle.

> If the future of the company is important to you, then don't hesitate to do what is necessary to save it.

Saving a business may require reducing the company's operations and curtailing expenses or even selling part of the business, but if that is what it takes to succeed, then don't falter in your steps. Play to win! Although bankruptcy no longer carries with it the 19th-century stigma of failure, it is a better image to be a moderately profitable entrepreneur than a formerly flamboyant and now bankrupt debtor.

A Guide to Terminating Operations

Once the decision to terminate an operation has been made, the steps involved are straightforward. Similar to taking inventory, termination is a process that can be systematized, and if all steps are followed, then desired results can be achieved.

Steps to Follow

1. Consider the effects.
   - Internal effects
   - External effects
   - Public relations
   - Media attention
2. Verify the financials.
   - Fixed assets, accounts receivable, and other assets
   - Liabilities: accounts payable, contractual liabilities, and leases
   - Current revenues and expenses

3. Determine the costs of terminating operations.
   - Payroll
   - Severance
   - Benefits
   - Final reimbursable expenses
4. Make decisions about personnel.
   - Employee layoffs
   - Reduced working hours
   - Salary reductions
   - Reutilization or transfer of employees
   - Lending or sharing of employees
   - Early retirement and voluntary separation
   - Temporary furloughs or temporary closings of operations
5. Reduce operations.
   - Temporary closings
6. Subcontract business.
   - Germinating subcontractors
7. Determine value to be recovered from termination.

Considering the Effects

Whether the company has decided to terminate all or just certain segments of the business, the process is the same. The first step is to meet with the company's senior managers and inform them of your decision. Listen to the company's managers. Be certain you understand all the possible effects and repercussions that terminating the operation will have on the company's remaining business.

Terminating operations has internal effects on the company as well as external effects based upon the perception that outsiders (vendors, customers, and the media) have after hearing the news.

Internal Effects

The internal effects are the results when viewed by the company's employees and operational management. Internal concerns include: decreased employee morale, the unavailability of terminated resources (personnel, production, parts inventory, etc.), and the underutilization of vacant real estate. Internal effects can also be beneficial and include the additional cash flow and capital that are potentially available for other more deserving areas of the business.

External Effects

The external effects of terminating operations are the results in the marketplace when viewed from the perspective of the company's customers, vendors, and competitors. These effects can include: lost revenues, reduced product offerings, continuing financial obligations, employee severance costs, contractual obligations, inability to hold market position, and a possible loss of formerly achieved strategic objectives (market share, key accounts, territory, etc.).

Public Relations

Don't ignore the public relations (PR) factor. How the termination is presented to those outside the company can greatly alter its impact upon the remainder of the business.

The effect on PR of terminating parts of the business can be positive, negative, or benign. Properly handled, the external view of the company might even be that management is exercising sound business judgment. At the worst, you want the view to be one of sympathy, with customers and vendors saying, "It's the economy," or "It's happening to everyone." What you want to avoid is projecting the image that the company is failing.

Remember that no one likes to hear bad news as a surprise. At the proper time, inform the company's customers, vendors, and employees about the company's plans for terminating operations. No one keeps bad news secret. Assume that if you tell one vendor or customer, the information will be known by all vendors and customers within a few days.

Work with the company's managers to prepare a short white paper listing commonly asked questions and answers

(Q&A) about the termination. Why is the company terminating the operation? When will it be effective? What does it mean to customers with back orders? Where should customers go for service? Spare parts? What will happen to the employees? When will suppliers be paid?

Make the Q&A simple and succinct, i.e., try to tell a story that a reasonable businessperson would believe. Put a contact name and telephone number on the Q&A to answer any additional questions. Provide the receptionist and managers with the Q&A. Post additional copies where most employees will have the opportunity to read it during the first day that it is posted. Send copies to other offices. The easiest way to avoid rumors is to answer the questions first, before the rumors start.

Media Attention

Be prepared for the media. (See Chapter 12 for a complete guide on how to control publicity of adverse announcements.) Designate one person in the company as the press contact and give the receptionist his home phone number. The press may not come; it depends how noteworthy the news is and what else happened that week. Don't go looking for media attention, but if the media knocks on your door, don't be caught napping.

Adopt the attitude of *Pravda*. (*Pravda*, which means "truth" in Russian, was the name of the major daily propaganda newspaper in the former Soviet Union.) The easiest way to dispel rumors is to promote your own version of the truth. If members of the press ask questions, don't be afraid to give them (or send via fax) a copy of the Q&A, or prepare a special Q&A for the press.

Avoid the consequences of negative publicity. These can include customers canceling orders, leaving the company with additional inventory, and vendors demanding immediate payment or failing to make deliveries.

Write a personalized letter to each vendor and customer who is affected. The letter should explain the reasons for the closing, the effective date, and what it will mean to the company's business relationship with them.

Verifying the Financials

An important step in the process of terminating or reducing an operation is to *quantify* and to *verify* the financials associated with the subject business. The required financials include: lists of fixed assets, accounts receivable, other assets, accounts payable, other liabilities, current revenues and expenses, the expected costs of terminating or reducing operations, and the value to be recovered from the operation.

Pre-existing financials should be disregarded when terminating a business. Remember the rule not to rely upon financials that were generated without your direct supervision. The assumptions that were made on the valuations of fixed assets, receivables, and inventory for taxes or previous financial statements are not very useful to the manager terminating all or parts of a business.

Fixed Assets

Obtain or compile a detailed and complete list of the fixed assets of the business to be terminated. *Detailed* means including serial numbers, manufacturers, and model numbers of fixed assets, where available. *Complete* means including all items that could be considered assets.

We have seen a Cadillac listed on the balance sheet at $6,000 because that was the balance remaining on the bank loan used to purchase the car. The same vehicle was later appraised for $15,000. We have also seen electronics shops with $50,000 of very marketable tools and equipment written off as improvements to real estate with no recoverable value.

> *Warning:* Do not rely upon the list of fixed assets unless the inventory was performed recently and you personally trust the competency and the loyalty of the managers who supervised the physical inventory.

The fact that an inventory or any financial report was performed under the supervision of a certified public accounting firm is no guarantee that the details are accurate. It means that the rules of the American Institute of Certified Public Accountants were supposed to have been followed, but most CPAs would agree that there is no substitute for a fresh and complete physical inventory of all assets.

Accounts Receivable

Create a complete list of *all* accounts receivable. Pay particular attention to accounts that were written off or marked uncollectible during the past twelve months. The A/R documents should include the credit information on each customer who has done business with the company during the past year, copies of all outstanding invoices, an aging report for each customer, and a summary report for all customers. (See Chapter 6 for a complete discussion on handling and collecting receivables.)

Other Assets

Do not neglect the search for other assets after locating all of those detailed on the balance sheet. The sale of assets no longer essential to the business of the company can be an important source of cash.

Richard Miller, former CEO of Wang Laboratories Inc., spent three years uncovering and selling nonstrategic assets to raise money to keep the company alive. After he took the helm in 1989, Miller sold nonstrategic assets and recouped more than $300 million to keep Wang out of bankruptcy court. Although his efforts could not stem the tide and the company eventually filed for reorganization in bankruptcy in late 1992, Miller had purchased three years of breathing room by the sale of assets unessential to the core business.

Don't forget about other assets. What about computer or office equipment in the personal possession of current or past employees? Spare parts and equipment at customer sites? Security deposits on utilities? Company-owned radios and cellular telephones? Deposits for mailings at the post office and mailing houses? Co-op advertising and promotional credits? Old bank accounts? Refunds for airline tickets? Insurance settlements? Advance deposits for trade shows and conferences?

Liabilities

The cardinal rule to remember when considering liabilities is that most can be renegotiated. Liabilities that are of concern to the business terminating or reducing operations are: accounts payable, contractual liabilities, leases, payroll-related liabilities, and current expenses.

- *Accounts payable.* Payables are bills the company needs to pay or renegotiate. When terminating or selling operations, don't make the mistake of overstating or understating the accounts payable. Read Chapter 5 carefully for instructions on how to verify payables and negotiate with vendors.

- *Contractual liabilities.* Contractual liabilities can include loan agreements, uniform delivery and laundry contracts, janitorial contracts, waste removal contracts, maintenance contracts, telephone answering services, security services, and blanket purchase orders. Although some of these businesses will initiate litigation to recover the damages incurred in early terminations of contracts, most are reasonable and will negotiate.

- *Leases.* Leases can be grouped into three basic categories: vehicle, equipment, and real estate. You must also consider whether the lease is an obligation of the corporation or if an officer or employee cosigned (personally guaranteed or accepted joint responsibility) for the obligation.

   The terms and conditions of leases are often the easiest liabilities to renegotiate for a business that is terminating operations. Evaluate your position and use your leverage when negotiating. Vehicle and equipment leases can be sold, renegotiated, or terminated. Leases for real estate are special cases, and it is wise to seek the assistance of a trained professional when renegotiating these types of agreements. For a complete discussion on leases for real estate, see Chapter 8.

   An experienced attorney should review each of the company's leases and identify the responsible parties and the order and trigger for each obligation. Analysis of obligations and guarantees relating to leases is also necessary to evaluate the results of a bankruptcy filing or insolvency proceeding.

For a complete discussion on vehicle leases, see the section on leases in Chapter 5.

Current Revenues

In terminating an operation, make a strong effort to collect on all current revenues. These revenues may be an important (and possibly critical) source of cash during the last few weeks or months of operations.

If customers have orders pending that have not been filled and the items are in inventory, then ship today. Do not delay. If orders are pending that are beyond the company's current capabilities or are not scheduled for delivery until too far into the future, then consider "selling" the order to a competitor or a colleague in exchange for a commission on the sale. Depending on the business, the company may not even have to inform the customer. Where it is necessary to inform the customer, an introduction from you may be all that is needed to pave the way to a sale and earn your company a commission.

Current Expenses

Once the decision has been made to terminate operations, you must begin trimming expenses everywhere. All purchases above a preset limit *must* be approved by one designated person. Don't let anyone convince you that the company can't operate with such severe constrictions. In 1984, the brokerage giant Merrill Lynch had such a poor year that assistant vice presidents were limited in spending authority to less than $50! You must impose direct control on all expenses rapidly. Look everywhere to reduce overhead and expenses.

Informing the staff that the company will be terminating operations is not sufficient to control expenditures. Employees will act as they have been trained. Senior management's view is that the office will be closing in thirty days and any surplus office supplies will be wasted. But the office manager's view is that if the supply room is low on inventory, then she needs to reorder. The office manager doesn't think about what will happen at the end of next month; it's not her job.

Reduce the number of outside telephone lines immediately. The company won't need any lines in two months' time, and at an average cost of $150 to $200 per line per month, telecommunications can be a significant part of fixed overhead. The company could probably eliminate one-third of its telephone lines with little impact on the business.

Cancel all employee travel, conventions, exhibitions, and car and gasoline allowances, and restrict the use of the corporate travel agency. Recall all but the absolutely necessary company credit cards and cancel all remaining charge account privileges (gas stations, office supplies, etc.). Cancel all orders for goods that have not been received. Reduce or eliminate all scheduled services such as pest control, janitorial, and landscaping.

Appoint one of your trusted lieutenants as the absolute master of the warehouse, loading dock, and shipping dock. All shipments arriving from vendors, unless they contain products that have already been sold to a customer, should be refused at the loading dock. Acceptance of new shipments will only increase the company's current liabilities.

Review Chapter 4 for a more complete discussion of the types of expenses that can be reduced or eliminated.

Determining the Costs of Terminating Operations

There is an old maxim that "It takes money to make money." This maxim should be rewritten for the business discontinuing an operation as "It can take money to stop losing money." There are many costs directly attributable to the termination of a business. These costs can include: severance and vacation payroll, advertising to sell inventory, security costs (locksmiths, night watchpersons, etc.), temporary storage facilities for corporate records and inventory, professional fees (legal, accounting, and consulting), outplacement fees, and penalties imposed for the early cancellation of leases and contracts (use worst-case assumptions).

Because of the company's plans, vendors will probably not extend credit or accept checks that haven't been certified, and many expenses will need to be paid in cash. Estimate the costs associated with terminating an operation and prepare for them.

Payroll, Severance, Benefits, and Final Reimbursable Expenses

Prepare a very liberal forecast of the costs of terminating employees. There are four areas of costs to be concerned about: payroll, severance, benefits, and final reimbursable expenses.

1. *Payroll.* Forecast payroll costs from now until the effective date of the employees' departure or the company's termination of operations. Include in the forecast any commissions earned and owed.

2. *Severance.* Some employees may be entitled to severance pay if required by company policy, union contract, or state or federal law. The company may have some flexibility with the timing and distribution of these payments, lump-sum versus payments over time. Be prepared for employees, upon hearing the news or rumor of a closing, to announce immediate retirement and be entitled to additional severance pay.

If the company can afford it, you may opt to offer employees additional severance based on the length of their employment. Although this can be expensive, the company can reap benefits from its sensitivity to the plight of discharged employees. *The more humane the treatment of those laid off, the less traumatic and harmful the effect will be upon the remaining employees.*

3. *Benefits.* The company needs to keep all basic benefits (health insurance, etc.) in effect until the end of operations. All employees must receive proper legal notice under federal COBRA rules that they can continue the existing coverage by making direct personal payments. The company's insurance agency may be able to help with recommendations for the administration of this program.

4. *Final reimbursable expenses.* Although the company is terminating operations, it may still owe additional benefits includ-

ing accrued tuition reimbursement, vacation pay, and sick pay. Issue a written policy to all employees that any requests for reimbursable expenses, travel, and entertainment *must* be received by the company within five business days. Use the memo to restate the company policy regarding receipts and proof of expenditures.

Making Decisions about Personnel

Although you should read Chapter 9, which covers the issues of personnel decisions in a troubled business thoroughly, the following are a few key rules that will help you.

1. Establish personnel objectives (reduce staff, reduce costs, or both).
2. Consider all the alternatives to layoffs to meet your objectives:
   * Reduced working hours
   * Salary reductions
   * Reutilization or transfer of employees
   * Lending or sharing of employees
   * Early retirement and voluntary separation
   * Temporary furloughs
   * Temporary closings of operations
3. Once the decisions have been made, be expeditious and firm in decisions to retain or terminate employees.
4. Where possible, always try outplacement of discharged personnel.

Employee Layoffs

Where redundancy is present or employees can be readily replaced, companies may choose to lay off portions of their staff. Although the economic cost can be minimal, the emotional cost of terminating employees can be significant.

Alternatives to Layoffs

Before making any decisions to lay off employees, first examine methods for reducing costs and increasing revenues. The following are a few alternatives to employee layoffs that are discussed fully in Chapter 9.

• *Reduced working hours.* Reducing the number of hours worked each week as an alternative to employee layoffs has been used as a method of reducing payroll costs by many Fortune 500 companies.

• *Salary reductions.* Some companies have opted to reduce salaries in particular jobs or across the entire company as a method of reducing payroll while avoiding terminating employees.

• *Reutilization or transfer of employees.* Employees can be demoted, downgraded, or transferred to other jobs. Any employees whom you want to use in other areas of the company or transfer to other offices should be informed immediately that a position is available and they only have a few days in which to make a decision.

• *Lending or sharing of employees.* An alternative to using the employee within the company is to place the employee with a customer or vendor on a temporary basis. This has been successfully done with technicians and customer service and training personnel, who can be lent or "rented" to customers or vendors for extended periods.

• *Early retirement and voluntary separation.* Many companies that have been reluctant to lay off staff have offered early retirement to their employees. Called voluntary separation, these packages can be combined with outplacement assistance to find the retirees new employment.

• *Temporary furloughs or temporary closings of operations.* Temporary furloughs for part of the workforce can include forced vacations or unpaid leaves of absence. The entire workforce is furloughed during a temporary closing.

To maintain company morale among those not laid off, many companies provide outplacement counseling for their discharged employees.

Reducing Operations

An alternative to terminating operations is to scale back and reduce production expenses that are necessary for, but separate from, the company's primary business. For some companies this can be done by subcontracting (also called farming out or outsourcing) or by reducing operational expenses.

There are many ways to trim operational expenses including: reducing the hours worked each week, temporarily closing facilities, laying off employees, moving to smaller facilities, subcontracting business, and selling subsidiary nonessential operations. Reducing production capacity is sometimes called downsizing, though new corporate missionaries are now calling it rightsizing.

Where the costs of operations can be immediately reduced by a temporary closing of facilities, the manager of a troubled company should carefully evaluate the option. This technique has primarily been used by large businesses, but small and medium-size companies may also find value in closing offices and facilities for several weeks during holiday or slow seasons.

Subcontracting Business

Subcontracting operations can reduce production costs and relieve a company of the problems associated with an uneven or cyclical flow of orders. It can also allow a company to focus its attention on its core business. By subcontracting the company may be able to recover some of the working capital invested in the operation by selling the excess equipment, inventory, and facilities.

A business can subcontract an operation to reduce costs and sometimes also recover value for the capital invested in the operation. A vending machine distribution business had constructed and was staffing an electronics repair shop with five employees, $50,000 in sophisticated test equipment, and $75,000 in parts. The company had witnessed a reduction in the volume of repair orders and found that the revenues from operating the repair facility no longer justified the expenses. The company subcontracted with an independent electronics shop to repair the products at a lower cost. The subcontractor agreed to purchase the company's test equipment and spare parts. This is an example of a win-win situation for both businesses.

Sometimes the idea to subcontract comes from a desire to concentrate the company's resources on its primary business. Drake Beam Morin, Inc. (DBM), one of the country's largest outplacement consulting firms, had grown quickly and found itself with high costs and management problems in the internal operation that produced manuals and printed materials for its clients. DBM subcontracted the printing services, resulting in lower costs and more time to focus on its primary business.

When subcontracting achieves lower costs and employees who would have been laid off are hired by the subcontractor, then the contractor, the management, and the employees are all winners. John Fluke Manufacturing Company was able to achieve this type of win-win-win victory. The company, which is synonymous in the engineering world with quality handheld meters, had grown steadily since its inception in 1948, and by 1992 an entire division was devoted to printing operations. As part of a restructuring and cost reduction program, Fluke terminated its printing operation and contracted with a local company to provide these services. Fluke was also able to outplace (find jobs for) six of its employees scheduled for layoffs. The results to Fluke were reduced costs, a subcontractor with employees who already knew the business, and little negative effect on company morale because of the outplacement.

Germinating Subcontractors

Sometimes you can "germinate" a small business to serve your company's needs and simultaneously reduce costs. Take the example of the automobile dealership that needed a paint and body shop for repairs. During the last few years, the company observed that the used vehicles it received were in better condition and only occasionally needed body work. The company could no longer justify maintaining a repair shop.

The dealership's owner helped a group of employees to establish an independent paint and body shop. He sold them the tools and equipment from his shop on favorable terms and guaranteed them 100 percent of the dealership's repair business. The dealership had achieved a win-win-win situation. It had reduced its costs, recovered good value for its assets, and outplaced a group of employees.

To provide jobs for its employees, Hewlett-Packard, known for its innovative personnel policies, recently germinated two small businesses from departments that were going to be reduced or terminated. The employees of these departments, which provided internal training and technical writing services to the company, accepted reduced salaries and benefits, but they did not have to face the prospect of unemployment.

Determining Value to Be Recovered from Termination

> *Warning:* Once the company has announced layoffs or the termination of an operation, it needs to monitor closely the warehouse and all facilities. Inventory, tools, and supplies have a way of disappearing under unusual circumstances following the notice of a facility closing. Don't hesitate to change the locks, hire security guards, and impose whatever new controls are necessary to preserve and protect the company's remaining assets.

Operations that are terminated or reduced usually have surplus assets that can be sold. Sell them today. Tomorrow the items will be worth less and the storage will be an additional cost. You can sell just about anything the company has as surplus: used office supplies, office furniture, fixtures, storage racks, packing and mailing supplies, cleaning supplies, inventory, spare parts, manuals, and computer software.

Make a list of all surplus assets and put approximate resale values on the items. Don't hold out on yourself. Why do you need three photocopy machines when you have reduced your staff to fifteen employees? Sell them! Sell anything you can. The cash value you recover is far more valuable today than the asset will be tomorrow.

8

Real Estate

The largest expense a company has next to payroll is the cost of facilities. This consists of two components: (1) the rent or mortgage payment and (2) the regular operating expenses of property taxes, insurance, utilities, maintenance, common area charges, cleaning, security, and landscaping.

The Good News

The good news is that because of the massive overbuilding of the commercial and industrial real estate markets of the late 1980s, there is excess supply in nearly every U.S. market. Vacancy rates for office space range from 27 percent in Dallas to 22 percent in Los Angeles and 20 percent in New York City.

As a result, it is strictly a buyer's/renter's market, so the negotiating power is in your hands. In most cases landlords will accept any reasonable restructuring or forbearance proposals. America is filled with retailers paying no rent for a year and postponing payments until the end of the lease or extending it a year. Businesses in office towers are regularly getting lower rents, postponements, and forbearance agreements, or they are moving to less space at lower cost in the same building with the aid of the landlord.

Industrial space is being converted to small business incubators, low-cost housing for the homeless, or flea markets. Even the IRS does not want industrial buildings. From Miami to Seattle, tens of millions of square feet of space sit vacant.

This is the best time in nearly fifteen years to renegotiate space-related overheads. Landlords would rather have a building that appears filled with tenants paying some rent, than one sitting vacant, making it unattractive to prospective tenants.

Most businesses, during their growth and expansion mode, took at least 20 percent extra space as a contingency allowance. Just as many businesses became overstaffed, most become "overspaced" as well. You can almost certainly make do with less space than you have now.

Few businesses audit their overall space costs. Retailers rarely check to see if mall owners are overcharging on common area costs and taxes. The bad news is that most are.

Attacking the Costs

Attacking the cost of real estate is critical to any survival plan, and the lessons learned should be remembered during the resurrection phase. Any would-be white knight investors, new lenders, or purchasers will look at real estate costs at the very beginning of their assessment. Getting these costs under control and in line is essential early in the survival plan to establish credibility. Creditors will view your downsizing of space as a tangible start in your efforts to accumulate and conserve cash to pay their bills or bank loans.

There are a number of alternative ways of reducing the cost of real estate. These methods include: closing locations, consolidating operations, negotiating a reduction of rent or mortgage payments, moving to a new location, or subletting some of your space.

Methods for Reducing Rent or Mortgage Payments

- Close locations.
- Consolidate operations.
- Negotiate a reduction in or forbearance on current payments.
- Renegotiate the terms and conditions of the lease.

- Move to a new location.
- Sublet some of your space.
- Reduce operating expenses and create less need for space.

Closing Locations

When contemplating the closing of a location or facility, answer the following questions: Do you really need each of your locations? Does the revenue generated from the location justify the cost of operating it? Do customers visit your office? Would customers be unwilling to travel to another of your locations?

As an alternative, could your employees travel to the customers' locations? Are you maintaining the location for image, for future business, or for additional revenue to the bottom line this year? How much business would you lose if you closed the office? Could you use alternative facilities to perform the same or similar operations at a lower cost? What additional costs would the company incur by operating the business from an alternative location?

With the movement to the telecommuting worker, fax machines, modems, and the mobile sales force, the fixed office headquarters is becoming more obsolete. One computer sales organization, fighting for survival in a cost-competitive market, reduced its regional offices in ten cities from 20,000 square feet to 2,000 with clerical staff, accounting, and a district sales manager. All full-time sales staff were given a suitcase containing a notebook computer, mini-fax, and cellular phone. All salespeople work out of their cars and homes and attend sales meetings at the office. Mail is directed to their homes. Office costs and related overheads have declined by nearly 60 percent despite the expenditure on the new computer hardware for the workers.

Clearly, the large fixed city center office is a phenomenon of the 1980s, not the 1990s. Many companies in their movement toward the vertical (hollow) organization have downsized middle management by as much as 25 percent. The 75 percent organization is more cost efficient, competitive, and productive. Most importantly, it uses less space, less clerical overhead, and less cash.

Moving While Under the Gun

The troubled company doesn't usually want to advertise a move. Letting the public know you are moving can be like ringing the alarm bell for creditors.

Although secrecy is not always necessary when planning a move, it can be advantageous in some situations. The best example of a secret move that was executed out of necessity with the precision of a clandestine military operation was the now famous (or, if you were a Baltimore fan, infamous) 1984 relocation of the NFL Baltimore Colts to Indianapolis. The day before the move, the Colts' owner, Robert Isray—who had been negotiating with several cities simultaneously either to move the franchise or stay in Baltimore—accepted Indianapolis's offer. What is not widely known is that both the Colts and Isray were also moving to escape their creditors.

While Isray was negotiating, the Maryland state legislature enacted a law permitting a municipality to hold onto a sports franchise by right of eminent domain. Isray was also in debt to the city government for back rent and to local banks for overdue loans. Isray's creditors had been patient and understanding of his pleas of poverty, but he suspected their patience would end if the Colts left Baltimore. All indications were that if the Colts announced their departure, the municipality, the state, and his creditors would attempt to block the move.

Early in the evening of March 28, 1984, executives of Mayflower Moving & Storage, working in concert with Isray, secretly dispatched fifteen moving vans and crews from cities all over the East Coast to the Colts' Maryland training complex. By 10 P.M., the trucks had arrived and the crews began loading their cargo. None of the drivers knew the final destination.

In the predawn darkness, the vans pulled out of the training facility loaded with all the property of a modern NFL team and headed west. Some of the drivers thought they were driving to Phoenix, which had been actively negotiating to obtain the Colts. It wasn't until they had crossed the Maryland state line that the drivers were informed that their final destination was Indianapolis.

The move was conducted with such secrecy that even the Colts' organization was not informed. According to eyewitnesses, the next morning, "Employees reported to work, and there was no furniture in the office, just a few telephones on the floor. . . . There was no equipment in the locker room. No weights in the weight room. . . . The men from Mayflower were thorough, they even took the dumbbells."[1]

Although the state of Maryland and the city of Baltimore continued to use the legal system to prevent the relocation of the franchise, once the team had physically left, the only game they could play was catch-up. The Colts had a winning season that first year in Indianapolis.

The lesson to be learned is that if your company needs to move in a hurry, in secret, and creditors and courts are close behind, call Mayflower. Just tell them you want the "Colts special."

Consolidating Operations

Consolidating multiple operations into the same location can often benefit the company by reducing the real estate costs of each operation and by eliminating any resulting overlaps in resources (human, equipment, vehicles, inventory, supplies, taxes, and overheads).

Can you consolidate some of the company's operations into other space already occupied by your company? Do you need to lease new space and consolidate multiple operations into one location? Could you share space with another company?

An example where consolidation of discrete operations reduced costs was an electronics manufacturer that maintained separate sales and service facilities. The sales office, located in a high-priced corporate office park, was used by the sales staff to make telephone calls, prepare for meetings, and store product samples and literature. The office space when originally leased was furnished nicely to project a professional image to the company's customers. However, the company had discovered that customers rarely visited the sales office and 90 percent of all sales were made by salespersons visiting the customer.

The service facility included underutilized space and was located in a mixed-usage light industrial park adjacent to the interstate highway. The company renegotiated its lease on the service facility and agreed to renew the lease for an additional five years in exchange for the landlord building a sales office (at no out-of-pocket cost to the company) in the front of the service facility.

The company moved the sales office into the service facility and significantly reduced its monthly real estate costs. The company also realized several additional benefits. The new facility was more conveniently located to the interstate highway and gave the salespersons quicker access to customers. The company could now place the product samples and literature in the existing stockroom with the proper inventory control procedures necessary to maintain adequate stocks. The company also realized cost savings by reducing the number of telephone lines required; by laying off one receptionist and one secretary; and by eliminating one fax machine, one photocopy machine, and one postage meter. There were also savings in taxes, maintenance, and stationary.

Many noncompeting professionals have consolidated together. Lawyers, accountants, consultants, financial planners, insurance agents, and engineers regularly consolidate in an office building sharing common reception, boardrooms, fax machines, photocopiers, clerical staff, and telephone systems. The net result is that all the professionals give the impression of large space and a prime location, but with shared common costs based on utilization, all pay less than if they were on their own.

We also see retailers placing boutiques within existing stores—"a shop in a shop"—to reduce costs and capitalize on traffic.

Consolidating and closing facilities for retailers or consumer service businesses is particularly conspicuous. When a retailer with six stores reduces the number to three, everyone notices, including customers and creditors. But we regularly counsel retailers that store consolidation in the 1990s is less damaging than it was five years ago. Consolidate the excess or unsalable inventory into a warehouse location and use the warehouse as a clearance center. You can normally get one month's lease to conduct the sale and it keeps the store image intact. It frees up all your own warehouse space and cleans out your store space quickly, without damaging the store image of your remaining outlets. Many retailers are also consolidating by establishing one superstore or warehouse branch instead of a dozen small locations.

It is easier to consolidate for retailers if they have common landlords who appreciate the need to survive. This means keeping the good stores open and paying the landlord rent while the nonperformers are closed.

For retailers in difficulty, consolidation is important as well as potentially dangerous. It signals to suppliers and competitors that there are difficulties, but in most situations it becomes a basic survival option.

Analyze the operations of each location, applying full corporate overheads to determine if there is a positive cash flow from operations. If the store generates a negative cash flow and there is no strategic reason such as profile to keep it open, then the location must be closed. It will save direct rental costs plus costs of supervision and inventory.

Long drawn out closing sales are not the answer. Our retail research shows that the two best options are to transfer inventory to other locations to reduce markdowns or to conduct a one week blowout sale to grab as much cash as possible. Both minimize system damage by reducing the negative visibility of a closeout sale.

When to Separate Operations

Sometimes the existing consolidation can result in higher real estate costs than operating the business from separate locations. In these situations the company can reap a cost savings by separating the operations into different locations.

Separation is most efficient where operations requiring significant amounts of low-cost space (warehouses and manufacturing facilities) are combined with retail or front office operations that require small quantities of expensive frontage or space.

An example of a business that entered a troubled period because of the high cost of maintaining consolidated facilities was a dry-cleaning business located in Manhattan. The family-owned organization operated a processing facility at its main midtown location and maintained five satellite drop-off locations elsewhere in Manhattan. The company was operating at full capacity but losing money every month. These losses were a result of the high fixed costs of paying rent for the main location. The company was operating the processing plant in a location where it was paying a high rent for retail frontage space.

Faced with imminent eviction for three months' past due rent on its main location, the company was forced to move. Because of the strong resistance of dry-cleaning customers to walk two blocks to a new location, the company feared losing its most valuable asset, its customers. All of the nearby alternative locations were either too expensive or not suitable for combined use as a retail location and a processing facility.

A consultant examining the troubles of the business recommended that the company separate the processing facility from the retail operation. The consultant suggested it lease a small retail space across the street from the current location as a new drop-off location, thereby maintaining a hold on current customers. The company located a dry-cleaning plant in the Bronx that had excess capacity and was willing to lease its plant and machinery to the company every night from 6 P.M. to 6 A.M. The results were that by separating operations, the company was able to reduce its costs without losing any customers.

Another illustration of separating operations is a California-based women's clothing manufacturer that maintained a New York City showroom combined with a small warehouse totaling 10,000 square feet in an expensive building frequented by the buyers for major retail stores. The company needed more local warehouse space but couldn't afford the expense. The cost of maintaining the present warehouse was already too high, and the company was in a period of financial difficulty. After considering its options the company moved its showroom to a smaller 3,000-square-foot space on a more desirable floor in the same building and moved its warehouse to a 12,000-square-foot space in an industrial building located on a nearby side street.

The result was that the company gained a better showroom and a larger warehouse at a total cost of less than half of the original combined facility.

Negotiating a Reduction in or Forbearance On Current Payments

Why is it often possible to renegotiate leases and mortgages? Because most lenders and lessors are reasonable and want your company to remain financially strong enough to continue as their customer.

Most businesspersons sign a lease or mortgage and assume that the only opportunity for them to change the terms and conditions is prior to the signing or upon renewal. *This is a myth.* The terms and conditions of property leases and mortgages, although fixed in writing as legal documents, are not carved in stone and can often be renegotiated to your company's benefit. The more troubled your business is, the greater likelihood you have of renegotiating the original terms and conditions. Landlords want tenants and some cash flow. Because of this, you can often negotiate to receive a reduction or forbearance on current real estate payments.

> *Reminder:* The cardinal rule of the troubled company is, if those you do business with (customers, vendors, banks, and lessors) will benefit more by your staying in business than by your closing, then you have leverage to negotiate with and should treat everything as negotiable.

Renegotiating the Terms and Conditions of the Lease

You can renegotiate a lease in any type of real estate market. In a market sparse with new tenants, the property owner will be very flexible to avoid having a vacant property. In a market flush with new prospective tenants, the property owner will be likely to look favorably upon an early termination of the lease where there exists the opportunity to gain a new tenant at a higher rent.

Start by examining the costs of your leases. At what cost

can you afford to remain in your present location? Is there enough time remaining on the lease for you to pay less rent now, during the troubled period, and more rent at the end of the lease? Is the lease renewable at the end of the year? You may be able to use an early renewal as an incentive for the landlord to agree to terms more favorable to the present financial condition of your business.

Is it simply a question of a few months of not paying rent to allow the company to stay alive for the next year? Ask the lessor to agree to grant you a forbearance for the next three months of rent and then stretch the payments for past due rent over the next three years.

Do you owe three months' back rent? Then include the three months owed (called a deficiency) in your negotiations. As long as you include the past due amounts in your negotiations, then the lessor believes it has some hope of recovery. You don't need to pay the past due rent; just include it in discussions.

Always keep the hope of future prosperity alive in negotiations. If you don't keep a positive outlook and keep hope alive, no one else will. Be realistic, but remain optimistic about the prospects for the future, if only the landlord would grant you these small favors.

Landlords in general are a reasonable lot. If you tell them in advance of your difficulties and communicate openly, forbearance is far more likely.

Some landlords may offer to allow you to move to less attractive space in the same building or mall. You are still at the same address so on the surface nothing has changed. Others may not be so pleasant and can become shrill and demanding. The benefits of the U.S. bankruptcy law put the landlord at a disadvantage. The net result is that the advantage is in favor of the knowledgeable tenant in today's real estate market.

Being Paid to Terminate a Lease

Even when you are several months behind in your rent payments there are possibilities for terminating leases to your company's advantage. You may be surprised that a landlord can be convinced to pay your company (yes, the landlord will pay you!)

to terminate a lease early when he can move in a new tenant at a higher rent.

When you agree to terminate a lease or to extend its term—whatever be the lessor's desire—you are giving the lessor something it wants and you will discover that terms can be changed, past due rent put aside, eviction proceedings halted, and monthly rental payments renegotiated.

Avoiding Defaulting on Mortgages

Contrary to the gothic horror stories, lenders don't usually want you to default on a mortgage, which would result in their foreclosing on the property. Lenders are not in the business of managing real estate. They are in the business of lending money for a secured interest in real property and receiving the money back in installments with interest.

Try not to wait until the mortgage holder has initiated foreclosure proceedings to communicate your desire to negotiate. Even if you can't make a full payment, don't despair. Most mortgage lenders only want to see some regular payment (they call it debt service) even if the payment is only for half the amount due.

• *What do lenders want?* Lenders want to see some debt service and they want to know that the underlying property is being maintained and will not lose its value. The lenders want to know that the mortgagee is doing everything it can to make full payments or, in the alternative, to rent or sell the property with the proceeds being paid to the lender. They want the insurance on the property kept up-to-date to protect their equity interest.

• *What should you ask lenders for?* Try asking the lender to agree to accept only the interest portion of the mortgage obligation with a forbearance on the principal payments for the next six or twelve months. After the end of the period agree to resume interest and principal payments and to have the missing principal added to the original mortgage amount.

If you need a three-month deferral of mortgage payments, then ask the lender to agree to a three-month forbearance and have the difference added to the original mortgage, i.e., extend the term of the mortgage a few months.

If you are moving and unable to make any significant payments to the lender, agree to list the property for sale or rental with a real estate agent. Ask the lender to recommend a realtor. Demonstrate to the lender that you are doing everything you can in good faith to turn around the situation to the lender's benefit.

Methods of Reducing Mortgage Payments

- Make payments of interest only, with forbearance on principal.
- Make payments on a quarterly basis instead of a monthly basis.
- Ask for forbearance of three months' principal and interest.
- Ask for full forbearance and list the property for rent or sale.
- Rent the property with direct assignment of rent to the mortgage holder and forbearance on any deficiency.
- Rent a portion of the property with direct assignment of rent to the mortgage holder and forbearance on any deficiency.
- Reschedule debt at new lower rates with a small penalty payment.

Unless you are asking for only a few months' forbearance in payments, when renegotiating a property lease or mortgage, it is *strongly recommended* that you seek the assistance of a trained professional. Ask your colleagues to recommend real estate professionals or lawyers with specialties in real estate who can assist you in renegotiating leases and mortgages. Only a professional knows what your rights are and how to protect your company from harm while renegotiating and legally confirming these types of arrangements so they will be durable for the future.

Warning: Whatever arrangement you make, be certain that the changes and conditions are agreed to in writing, so you are not suddenly faced with an eviction or foreclosure pro-

ceeding because the lessor or mortgage holder changed its
mind. Retailers have less flexibility and their landlords may
act more quickly to close the business.

Moving to a New Location

You may evaluate your current location and decide either that
there is no way to cost-effectively utilize the property or that the
landlord will not negotiate a satisfactory reduction in rent. Then
move! Don't delay and don't wait until the landlord sends you
an eviction notice. Your objective is to locate your company
where you can make a profit.

Breaking Leases

Although the landlord can use the legal system to seek a judgment against your company for rent past due and can include
claims for damages for early termination of the lease, don't lose
any sleep over his waving of spears. Most landlords' barks are
far worse than their bites. They may threaten litigation but rarely
take the recourse except for eviction proceedings. Primarily they
want tenants who pay the rent on time, do not complain, and
lease in an orderly manner.

Although landlords threaten to change the locks on the
doors and to refuse you permission to move out, these are not
usually powers that are within their legal rights. Refusing to permit your company to move or holding your property can subject
landlords to significant liability for the loss to your business and
possible criminal charges for "conversion," the legal term for
taking your property and treating it as their own.

Landlords know that courts do not view as high-priority
cases litigation for damages based on early termination of leases,
particularly those where the tenant has already vacated the
space. These cases languish in the court dockets for years. A
reasonable real estate attorney can raise defenses on your behalf
and use the state rules of civil procedure to delay the landlord's
day in court for at least a year and possibly as long as three
years. The landlord must act to mitigate his damages by trying
to rent the space and reduces his losses.

Every month that goes by is another month that you can work on rebuilding your business and another month that the landlord must continue paying his lawyer to pursue a legal remedy. Even when the landlord gets to court, if you have defenses such as a leaky roof or insufficient heating or air-conditioning, you may have offsets against the amount you owe the landlord. Furthermore, at any time prior to judgment being issued, you can instruct your counsel to negotiate an out-of-court settlement with the landlord.

In summary, if you have to break a lease because you have no alternative, then do it! Try to negotiate, but if the results are not sufficient to keep the company alive, then walk. Walk away quietly and discretely, but walk away.

Where to Move

As a financially distressed company, don't look for a new long-term lease when moving. You may not find the optimal space. Instead, find space that works for you. Do you need back office space, a warehouse, or a manufacturing plant? Can you share space with another company? Take a month-to-month rental if you must. It might cost a little more in the short term but gives you no fixed obligation.

Move to a property that works for you, not for your dreams of what might have been. It is better to move to a low-cost space for a year and then move to a more attractive space when you have completed your business recovery. After you have moved once, moving a second time will take considerably less effort.

How to Move

When moving under threat of eviction or other debtor-creditor–related litigation, plan the move very carefully. Start cleaning up and packing as much as possible in advance, but do not give the appearance that you are packing.

Plan the move well and be certain you take everything with you when you leave. Once you have vacated the premises, expect that the landlord will change the locks or post a security guard within a few hours.

Do's and Don'ts of Moving

The following is a list of do's and don'ts for troubled companies planning a move while under the gun of one or more creditors.

Do's

- *Do* advise your attorney that you may need her services on the day of the move. This way you will have counsel available if the landlord denies your company access to the freight elevator or bars the doors.
- *Do* have cash available to take care of tips for elevator operators, local security guards, and porters.
- *Do* hire a moving company from the other side of town.
- *Do* prearrange for your telephone lines to be automatically switched to your new location.
- *Do* give the post office a letter in writing requesting that all mail for the company be held at the post office for one week.
- *Do* change your bank accounts

Don'ts

- *Don't* advise the landlord that you will be moving.
- *Don't* advise your customers and vendors you will be moving. You'll have plenty of time to inform them later.
- *Don't* fill out a change-of-address card at the post office in advance.

If you own too much furniture or equipment for your new location, then try to sell as much as you can. Place what you can't sell in storage in one of the now commonplace rent-a-room storage facilities that can be leased for $25 to $50 per month.

Subletting Some of Your Space

If it's not possible to move or if the cost of relocating is too expensive, consider subletting or renting a portion of your space. If your lease does not permit you to sublet the space, do it anyway. As long as the landlord is receiving rent, he is unlikely to be concerned about your subletting space.

Your ideal tenant is a company in a related or possibly complementary business. Avoid any company that competes with the business of your company. Try approaching some of your vendors or customers as potential subtenants. Consider what you have to offer a prospective tenant; he may be interested in sharing secretarial services, a receptionist, conference rooms, or warehouse space. If you have a sales office, consider approaching companies that don't have one in your geographic area. Professional companies can usually share space with other noncompeting professional companies and can even refer business.

You may not need a long formal agreement with your tenant, but you do want a security deposit. Don't accept a check from the tenant unless it can be cashed before the tenant moves in. You don't want to find your company in the same position as your landlord.

Consider the type and quality of tenant you are looking for very carefully. Always check a tenant's past references. One horror story concerns a subtenant who, after the first month, came in one weekend with a truck and cleaned out the original tenant's warehouse and was never heard from again. A well-chosen tenant can be a savior. The wrong tenant can be the kiss of death. Make the sublet work for your company.

Reducing Operating Expenses and Creating Less Need for Space

As an alternative to moving or as a supplement to other cost reductions, most companies can reduce operating expenses associated with their real estate. You can reduce operating expenses by curtailing, economizing, or eliminating the following expenses: utilities, lights, security, landscaping, waste removal, and office cleaning.

To economize on HVAC (heating–ventilation–air-conditioning), install thermostats with timers in locked boxes. If you currently have maintenance contracts on the HVAC system, you may want to explore changing to a time and materials arrangement to reduce costs.

Designate an employee to make certain that all windows and doors are kept closed. Instruct employees to turn off power on all computers, copiers, and electric equipment on evenings and weekends.

> *Warning:* Do not eliminate your property insurance. You
> may want to increase the deductibles, but keep the policy
> in force. See Chapter 4 for suggestions on how to reduce
> insurance costs, but do not eliminate coverage.

Note

1. Dan Shaughnessy, "Ache Remains Where Colts Once Played," *Chicago Tribune*, October 11, 1992, p. C7.

9

Personnel

The first place that managers look to save money is payroll. Managers know if they fire employees they will reduce their labor costs. However, the problem of how to reduce costs without crippling the company's productivity does not have such easy solutions. Although layoffs produce initial savings, companies often pay a higher price in the costs of the trauma to the surviving business.[1] Our research shows that layoffs can result in loss of morale, declining customer service, less innovation, and loss of worker loyalty.

Many companies in the United States and in Europe have used alternative personnel management strategies to successfully reduce labor costs and avoid involuntary layoffs. These alternatives include shortening the workweek, reducing salaries, demoting or transferring employees, and offering voluntary job sharing, limited duration furloughs, and early retirement incentives.

However, in two recent surveys, fewer than half of the U.S. companies that laid off employees in the late 1990s considered all of the alternatives first.[2] There appear to be two reasons for this myopia: (1) Managers may not be familiar with alternatives to layoffs and (2) in times of crisis, managers are averse to risk.

This chapter discusses the various alternative employment strategies available to troubled companies with examples of how other businesses have successfully used them to reduce costs while maintaining company morale and productivity and improving profitability. The traditional method of reducing labor costs—involuntary termination (i.e., firing)—is treated with a step-by-step humanistic approach to managing the termination.

Change Can Be Good

Before the turmoil of the last ten years of downsizing and rightsizing destroyed a prevalent illusion, many managers and employees acted under the impression that a good job, once found, was their privilege for life. If managed properly, correcting this falsehood can have very positive effects upon the surviving employees. Once employees are reminded that their job security rests with the profitability of the company, they begin to think differently.

A study by Arthur Andersen Consulting says of the survivors of corporate layoffs, "They begin to ask management difficult and direct questions: What are you doing to become more competitive? What are your plans for success? How do you plan to turn the company around?"[3] We won't try to convince you that troubles are good for companies, but after reading this book you may agree that if the solutions to the troubles are well managed, the result can be a stronger company.

There are three basic methodologies for reducing labor costs: (1) reducing employee benefits, (2) exploring alternatives to layoffs, and (3) terminating employees. This chapter explores these methods and discusses how companies have used them to reduce costs.

Reducing Benefits

Sometimes, a company can be mistaken about the need to lay off employees to reduce costs. Employees' salaries and wages are only one element of the cost of labor: Employee benefits can represent an additional cost of 10 to 50 percent of labor costs. By carefully evaluating, pruning, and trimming benefits, personnel costs can be reduced without the need to reduce staff. The

W. M. Mercer and Associates 1994 Benefits Survey shows that 50 percent of employers are currently reviewing pension costs and 60 percent are reviewing benefits and salary costs.

This section explores the true costs of employee benefits packages and shows managers how to reduce these costs and instill in the employees an appreciation for the value of the benefits they are receiving.

Some Background on Benefits

Contrary to common belief, most businesses are under no legal requirement to provide any benefits other than unemployment and workers compensation insurance. The primary reason for providing benefits is to be competitive in the marketplace for hiring and retaining the best employees. A good benefits package attracts good employees and is considered indicative of how a company's management feels about its workforce.

Classical capitalists trying to maximize profits pose the question, "What is the optimal level of benefits that, when provided to employees, maximizes their productivity?" Unfortunately, the answer is not as simple as the question.

A company has three constituencies: its employees, its shareholders, and its customers. Which constituency is the most important? Is the goal of the company to maximize return to its shareholders? Is the goal to provide the best quality service to its customers? Is the goal to compensate employees to keep them happy and productive? Balancing the demands of the various constituencies with the company's strategic objectives is a difficult task.

All of the goals mentioned may be necessary for a company to be successful, but the problem is that some goals can be achieved only at the cost of missing the mark on others. When making decisions on layoffs, alternatives to layoffs, and changes to employee benefits, management is defining the company's strategic objectives.

Gil Amelio, CEO of National Semiconductor Corporation, who made the difficult decision to reduce benefits and lay off more than 5,200 employees, said, "It's a terrible mistake if you only manage a company for one constituency. . . . To keep people employed on a long-term basis, you have to do some painful things. Otherwise, there won't be any jobs at all."[4]

When informed by experts that they need to reduce employee benefits, most troubled companies respond that they couldn't possibly do it without losing valuable employees. This is another myth that managers hide behind. Although benefits are an important part of compensation, most employees would choose to keep their current jobs with reduced benefits instead of being unemployed. So remember: No benefits are inalienable rights and all are open for inspection.

Methods for Reducing Labor Costs

1. Reduce employee benefits.
2. Explore alternatives to layoffs.
3. Terminate employees.

Two Types of Employee Benefits

Benefits can be separated into two categories: visible (direct) benefits and invisible (hidden) benefits.

Visible benefits are those perks and fringes that employees view as part of the compensation package. These are the benefits that people consider when comparing your company with another job opportunity. These benefits can include health, life, and disability insurance; sick leave; vacation days; company-provided automobiles or automobile allowances; pension plans; retirement plans; subsidized education and training programs; and other company services provided for the express benefit of the employees.

Invisible benefits are products and services that your company provides to your employees, knowingly or unknowingly, where the employee benefits. These benefits include the employees' personal use of company-provided telephones, mails, couriers, fax machines, and photocopy machines. It also includes subsidized health care services (company nurse and/or physician), subsidized food services, coffee and soda service, and travel discounts. Employees are rarely aware of the full costs to the company of providing these invisible benefits and as a result are typically not appreciative of the value they receive.

Visible Benefits

Reducing Health Insurance Costs

The largest expense for companies providing employee benefits is usually health insurance. Most companies offer some form of health insurance with typical costs of $200 to $400 per employee per month. This coverage can be divided into five types of insurance: (1) basic medical and hospitalization, (2) major medical, (3) dental, (4) disability, and (5) life. Most companies require the employee to pay some portion of the premium, which is called a copayment.

Before taking steps to reduce your health insurance costs, you should examine your current coverage. Examine your plan and compare it to other available plans. If you haven't evaluated the insurance benefits you offer your employees in the last two years, you should. You will find that you can probably reduce insurance costs without significantly changing the coverage offered to your employees.

In examining your current benefits package, ask yourself the following questions: Is the company's offering competitive in the industry or geographic area? Can the company afford to continue the benefits package in its current form? Would it be better to reduce benefits or lay off employees? Are the employees really benefiting from and satisfied with the current plan?

Although health insurance is one of the key benefits that employees consider before deciding on a job, don't be mistaken that your company is *required* to provide insurance. Many small and midsize companies do not provide any insurance benefits, and recently some companies have either significantly reduced benefits or eliminated insurance altogether.

Regis Corporation, a company that operates more than 1,000 hair salons with 14,000 employees, recently eliminated all health care benefits to its employees citing as a reason that "the cost just got ridiculous."[5]

Try to determine whether your employees are satisfied. A manufacturing company with one hundred employees offered excellent medical insurance coverage and the employer generously paid 100 percent of the premium for both employees and their dependents. The plan included an annual deductible of $500 per person or $1,000 per family. After the deductible had been reached, the policy paid 80 percent of the costs of treatment and hospitalization. The cost to the company ranged from $200 per month for an employee to $400 per month for the employee and his or her spouse and dependents. Medical insurance costs to the company were approximately 15 percent of payroll costs.

Experiencing severe economic distress, the company hired a consultant to help identify areas in which to concentrate cost-reduction efforts. There was unanimous consent among managers that the benefits package was excellent and that all employees were satisfied with the coverage.

The consultant suggested evaluating the current policies and considering alternative coverage to reduce the costs of providing health insurance. Senior management was adamant that any significant change in the benefits package would have a disastrous effect on the company's workforce. The managers believed many loyal employees would leave if the company changed its insurance plan. The consultant agreed to examine the problem and deliver a report to management in two weeks.

The next day the secretary assigned to the consultant telephoned to say she would not be coming to work because she had to take her young son to the doctor. The following day the consultant asked how her son was feeling and what the doctor had told her. She responded that it was just a common cold but that every visit to the city's public health clinic required a long wait. Puzzled about why the employee used a city clinic, the consultant asked why she wasn't covered by the company's medical insurance. She responded that she was covered but that she earned only $24,000 per year and couldn't afford the $1,000 deductible for family coverage.

Since the secretary was new to the company, the consultant asked how she knew which clinic to visit. She said the employees in the warehouse had told her where to go and that they also used the public health clinics instead of the insurance coverage.

To determine who was benefiting from the company's health insurance coverage, the consultant requested the insurance carrier to provide a confidential list of the benefits received by each employee of the company during the previous year. He compared this list to the annual salary of each employee.

The results were not what management had represented at the meeting. With a few exceptions for hospitalizations and two cancer patients, employees earning less than $30,000 per year rarely used the medical insurance benefits. Over half of the total benefits claimed by the company had been received by the top 25 percent of the company's salary earners.

During the remainder of the interviews that the consultant conducted, employees were canvassed regarding their satisfaction with present health benefits. The lower-salaried employees and all of the hourly employees complained that the deductible was too high and that although the insurer paid claims rapidly, it was on a reimbursement basis and advancing the funds for medical services often presented a financial hardship for them.

After considering the demographics of the workforce and tabulating the results of the interviews, the consultant met with several insurance agencies to explore alternatives to the present plan. The consultant then made the following three recommendations:

1. The company should offer employees an option of continuing with the current insurance or joining a health maintenance organization (HMO). Forty-three of the one hundred employees signed up for the HMO option, resulting in an annual cost savings to the company of $35,000.
2. Employees should share the insurance cost with a weekly contribution of 25 percent of the premium—a copayment. The copayments resulted in annual cost savings to the company of $65,000.
3. Copayments would also force employees to shop between their coverage and that offered by their spouses'

employers (if spouses were employed and covered). Fifteen employees elected to be covered by their spouses' insurance or declined coverage. This resulted in annual cost savings to the company of $50,000.

From annual health insurance costs of $350,000, the company was able to reduce costs by $150,000, or a savings of approximately 43 percent.

Although there was discontent among employees at the initiation of copayments, the benefits package remained competitive in the industry and for the geographic area. Most other companies in the area had already introduced some amount of employee copayment. Overall, the majority of the employees were more satisfied with, and had a greater appreciation of, the benefits they were receiving.

How to Reduce Health Insurance Costs

1. Increase employee contributions for premiums.
2. Eliminate or reduce employer payments of premiums for spousal and dependent coverage and dental, disability, and life insurance.
3. Change to a higher deductible.
4. Change type of policy or insurance carrier.
5. Change policy to meet changing demographics of the workforce.
6. Increase waiting period for new hires to receive coverage.
7. Give employees options.

Increase Employee Contributions for Premiums

Typical employee contributions, or copayments, toward premiums for health insurance range from zero to 50 percent of the premium cost, depending on the geographic area and the industry. In today's economy, a contribution of around 25 percent is competitive.

If providing health benefits costs the company 10 percent of salary costs and the company institutes a 25 percent copayment plan, the result will be annual savings of at least 2.5 percent of payroll costs. In a company with a $2 million annual payroll, savings of 2.5 percent is equivalent to $50,000 per year, which could easily represent two employees' jobs that were saved.

Hawaiian Air, which has been hit hard by increased airline competition, needed to reduce operating costs. The company recently instituted a cost reduction plan that includes copayments for employee health insurance. The company's president said, "We're taking [these] steps now to reduce costs to be able to offer low fares and remain profitable."[6]

Eliminate or Reduce Employer Payments of Premiums For Spousal and Dependent Coverage And Dental, Disability, and Life Insurance

Eliminating employer contributions for spousal and dependent coverage may seem drastic for employers who perceived themselves as benevolent parents to their employees, but the continued existence of the company may be at stake. In the previous example of the manufacturing company with one hundred employees, fully eliminating any employer contributions for spousal and dependent coverage would have resulted in additional savings of almost $75,000.

Pro Fasteners, a medium-size parts distributor in Washington, D.C., needed to cut costs to remain competitive. The troubled company had historically paid for health insurance for its employees and their dependents. To reduce costs while avoiding layoffs, the company decided to purchase insurance coverage only for employees. Employees could continue coverage for their dependents, but the cost would be deducted from their paychecks. The results were cost savings and the departures of some employees, but the company was able to weather the storm and remain competitive.

Dental insurance is a great benefit for older employees and employees with children, but it is of lesser importance to young and single or middle-aged employees. Although some forms of dental insurance can be obtained without a group, they are not as comprehensive and have lower maximum benefit limits. To reduce costs, have employees pay the majority (if not 100 percent) of the dental insurance premium through payroll deduction and allow them to choose whether they want to be covered.

Metro Bolt & Fastener, a small hardware distributor in Detroit, was forced to consider ways to reduce costs to remain profitable in a sluggish economy. The company took two actions related to employee benefits: (1) The company switched insurance carriers and (2) employees were asked to pay for the formerly company-paid dental insurance benefit. According to the president and founder, "It's a matter of survival. You can be increasing sales, but if your salary, maintenance, and administrative costs are rising faster, you're in trouble."[7]

Disability and life insurance are big luxuries to a distressed company. Those employees who wish to continue these benefits must pay the full cost.

Change to a Higher Deductible

Typical annual health insurance deductibles were once $100 to $300 per person. With the rising costs of providing health insurance, most policies have increased the annual deductibles to $300 to $500 per person. Examine your company's current policy and ask your insurance broker what the cost savings would be of increasing the annual deductible on your health insurance. The policy may be flexible enough to provide employees with the option of selecting a low or high annual deductible. If the option is available, have the employee pay any additional costs for a lower deductible.

Delta Air Lines, as part of its current program to cut costs by $1 billion, has reduced medical benefits for employees by increasing deductibles from $100 to $150 and increasing the maximum out-of-pocket expense.

Increasing the annual health insurance deductible per person can result in cost savings of 5 to 10 percent of annual premiums.

Change Type of Policy or Insurance Carrier

Group health insurance includes coverage for one or more of three categories of providers: any-provider, preferred provider organization (PPO), and health maintenance organization (HMO).

1. *Any-provider coverage* is usually the most expensive type of coverage and either pays for or reimburses up to a fixed fee schedule or fixed percentage of the amount charged by the medical professional of the employee's choice.

2. *PPO coverage* pays for the medical services *only* when the employee uses health professionals who are members of the plan. These professionals have usually agreed to a fixed fee schedule for the services they provide. Because of the reduced fee schedule, PPOs are less expensive than the any-provider coverage.

3. *HMO coverage* is now available in most metropolitan and some rural areas. Originally formed as cooperative health care organizations without a profit incentive, they can now be operated as either commercial or nonprofit businesses. HMOs provide medical and hospitalization services to their members, who usually pay a nominal copayment for each visit ($5 to $10 per doctor visit, $50 to $100 per hospitalization, and $2 to $5 per prescription). There is usually no annual deductible and no maximum lifetime benefit. The major limitation of HMOs is that members can receive their benefits only from professionals and medical facilities that are members of the HMO. Because of this limitation, HMOs are usually the least expensive type of coverage.

The last few years have seen the introduction of hybrid health insurance policies that provide both the company and the insured with options for one or more categories of providers. One example is a policy that pays 80 percent of medical expenses when the employee uses a health professional who is a member of the PPO, but with the option for the insured to use any provider. However, the policy pays only 60 percent of expenses when the insured uses a health care provider who is not a member of the PPO. Another example would be a group policy that provides PPO coverage with an option for employees to elect HMO coverage.

With all the types of group health insurance available, companies should shop around to find the policy that best addresses the company's financial position and the health needs of its employees. The shopping expedition should include exploring new insurance brokers and carriers as well as different plans with the current carrier.

Change Policy to Meet Changing Demographics Of the Workforce

Examine the demographics of the company's workforce and employees' historical use of benefits. For example, if you have a mostly older workforce, where maternity benefits are less important, you may want to consider a less expensive policy with reduced maternity benefits. A company whose employees include many young parents may prefer a policy with stronger coverage for pediatrics and prescription medications. Where the employee costs for benefits are increased, but the insurance coverage is better tailored to the employee needs, it may prove easier to swallow.

Increase Waiting Period for New Hires to Receive Coverage

Some companies provide benefits to the employee from the first day of hire. Others have a probationary period, during which the new employee receives only a minimum of benefits. This waiting period is usually to allow both the employee and the employer to be certain there is a good fit.

The additional value to the company of a waiting period is the cost savings from not having to provide full benefits for a few weeks or months. This is particularly relevant to retail and service companies, where employee turnover rates exceeding 20 percent per year are typical.

Exhibit 9-1 shows the possible effects of implementing a waiting period for insurance eligibility for new hires. Instituting a two-month waiting period for health insurance eligibility for new hires reduces the cost of providing insurance for that em-

Exhibit 9-1. Effects of implementing a waiting period for insurance eligibility for new hires (assuming annual employee turnover of 20 percent).

Waiting Period	Percentage Annual Savings per New Employee	Percentage Annual Total Savings for Company
1 month	8.3	1.7
2 months	16.7	3.3
3 months	25.2	5.0

ployee, during the first year, by almost 17 percent. For a company with a 20 percent annual turnover of employees, this policy of waiting two months for insurance eligibility would result in total annual savings of 3.3 percent of the cost of providing group medical insurance.

Give Employees Options

As a policy it is politically unwise to eliminate types of insurance coverage altogether; rather, where available, the employer should provide for the option to allow the employee to continue uninterrupted coverage by directly paying the entire premium herself or by purchasing alternative or replacement coverage. This coverage can be purchased through payroll deduction using pretax dollars under current tax regulations.

The employer can also arrange with independent insurance agents to meet with each employee on an individual and confidential basis to provide the employee with a variety of options for her to purchase replacement and alternative coverage. One employer we know was forced to significantly reduce all employer-provided insurance coverage. The company provided an office, on site, three mornings a week for an independent insurance agent to meet with interested employees during business hours to discuss replacement and alternative coverage.

Reducing Other Types of Benefits

Although it is never easy to tell employees that they will be receiving less in their paycheck, the pain can be eased by using a positive approach when informing them. By explaining the need for starting or increasing copayments in a positive way, as a method to save jobs and avoid layoffs, you may ease the acceptance of and reduce employee resentment of the new policy.

It can also be useful to compare the company's benefits to those offered by other similar companies in the industry or the area and demonstrate to employees that your benefits plan is still competitive.

Sick Leave and Vacation Pay

Vacation and sick leave affect both a company's balance sheet and its cash flow. In the long run, employees accumulating large quantities of vacation and sick leave add to the liabilities listed on the balance sheet and decrease the value of the company. However, in the near term, a company may want to deter employees from taking vacation during a critical period when their absence would directly affect the company's productivity and revenues.

Start by projecting the company's work flow for the next six months. If the company experiences a particularly slow period between Christmas and New Year's Day or during the last two weeks of August, you may want to ask that all employees take their vacation during that period.

If the situation is critical enough, you may also want to ask even those employees who have not accrued vacation time to take an unpaid vacation. If the policy is presented as being for the good of the company, most employees will accept it. How you present the policy to your employees in large measure determines their response.

It can be less expensive for the company to insist as a matter of policy that employees use their vacation time each year and not carry over unused vacation leave for subsequent years. An employee who uses accrued vacation time long after earning it costs the company more than the original value of the benefit if the employee's salary or value to the company has increased in the interim.

Remember that no benefits are sacred cows. Future vacation and sick leave are not divinely ordained rights. They are benefits given to employees for the company to remain competitive. Although it may appear to be difficult to reduce benefits for long-time employees, remember that these are the same employees who derived considerable benefit from the company's liberal policies during more prosperous times.

Start by instituting new rules for leave. With advance notice of a few months, advise all employees in writing that they will not be permitted to carry vacation and sick leave from year to year unless there are extenuating circumstances. The policy should be that all accrued leave must be used within twelve months of being earned.

Another common problem is that the highest salaried employees are the most likely to take longer vacations. In a troubled period there is nothing wrong with advising *all* employees, particularly management-level employees, that they cannot schedule more than five consecutive vacation days. Most will be motivated to stay for fear of losing their jobs while they are away.

Be wary of excessive sick leave. A simple but rigid policy of requiring a note from the employee's physician for more than two consecutive days of sick leave reduces the abuse by dishonest employees without causing hardship to the honest ones. Companies may want to relax this rule during a period of flu or other common medical disorder. The results of a stringent sick leave policy are cost savings and increased productivity.

Pension Plans

Employer contributions to pension plans are not inviolate. In May 1994, General Motors announced plans to contribute $10 billion of stock and cash to reduce the estimated $20 billion they owe the pension plan that benefits more than 600,000 current and former GM employees.[8] Total underfunding of the 65,000 employee benefit pension plans in the United States at the end of 1993 reached a record of $54 billion up from $38 billion in

1991 and \$27 billion in 1987.[9] Although it is unlikely that your deficiencies will be as great as those of GM, there is certainly ample precedent to be in the position of owing money to your employee pension plan. Borrowing from your employees' future to help keep your company alive should not be your first choice, but if it becomes necessary, make the prudent choice.

Retirement Benefits

Who told you that the company must provide retiree health benefits? According to a 1993 study of more than 1,000 companies,[10] 72 percent of very large companies (those with more than 5,000 employees) provide retiree health benefits, but only 37 percent of midsize companies (those employing 200 to 999 workers) provide similar coverage. Furthermore, for the midsize organizations, the percentage providing coverage had declined from 44 percent in 1992. The study reveals that even the percentage of large firms (1,000 to 4,999 workers) offering retiree coverage is only 52 percent. The results of this study for the troubled company are that it doesn't need to offer retiree health benefits to remain competitive.

The study also showed that 80 percent of all retiree health benefits plans now require some copayment by the retiree. Contrast this statistic with that of a previous study that showed that in 1985, most retirees who received health benefits did not pay any portion of the cost. Copayment for retirees has become widespread in a relatively short period of time.

For the troubled company this means that if it hasn't already implemented a copayment plan for retiree health care benefits, now is the time to implement one. In addition, instituting a copayment program or increasing the amount of copayment will not make the overall benefits package uncompetitive.

Subsidized Education

Most troubled companies should reduce or at least temporarily suspend all subsidies for education. Companies can suspend subsidies for a semester or two with a statement that the

Courier Services

Employees and managers can easily avail themselves of the company's accounts for messengers, UPS, Federal Express, etc., and use them for personal mail and packages. Don't let it happen. Inform managers it will not be tolerated, and most importantly audit the invoices you receive from the couriers. A few well-timed audits—for example, just after Christmas—will result in identifying the abusers and sending the proper message to the rest of the company that the practice will not be tolerated.

How to Detect Abuse

The single best piece of advice that anyone can give you to detect abuse of invisible benefits is to audit the company's invoices. Usually the abuses are not hidden and are glaringly obvious; it's just that no one is looking. Emphasize to all managers the need to review and approve invoices before the company will pay for them.

If you are suspicious of the abuse of photocopy machines, fax machines, or postage meters, there is an easy method for detecting the abuse since these machines usually have mechanical or electronic counters. Since most of the abuse is done after hours, it is easy to detect. Leave the machine unlocked and have an honest employee keep a logbook of meter readings at the end of every day and the beginning of the next day. Although you will probably detect the abuse, you may not know the name of the abuser. Don't worry about it. As stated frequently in this book, the objective is to control costs, not punish employees.

If abuse occurred, it was because management either didn't care, wasn't looking, or tolerated it. The objective of a company in trouble is to control costs and improve management, not to point the finger of blame. (See Exhibit 9-3.)

Subsidized Services and Company Discounts

Subsidized services are subject to two problems: (1) abuse and (2) lack of appreciation by employees. Abuse can be controlled

Exhibit 9-3. Humor in the troubled company, or *de minimis curat lex* (the court does not consider trivial matters).

We are reminded of three examples where senior management wasted precious time looking for perpetrators of minor expense abuses, as if the individuals had committed felonies, instead of improving junior management and changing the procedures to prevent future abuse. We relate these stories for your amusement as well as to remind you that management talent is a valuable asset to waste.

Case 1: In *The Caine Mutiny* by Herman Wouk, the captain, although admittedly paranoid, spent several months searching for the perpetrators of the theft of strawberries from the refrigerator in the officers' dining room. The captain was convinced there was a duplicate key to the refrigerator, but he never suggested the lock be changed or the mess sergeant assume responsibility for vigilance over the fruit.

Case 2: A garment manufacturer filed for bankruptcy protection as a result of reported accounting irregularities. The problems were relatively serious for a public company: All that management (apparently) did was to report millions of dollars of profits for years, when it had a loss! Yet what did management concern itself with at a meeting the week before the bankruptcy filing? Not the false financial statements but the shortages that had been detected in the coin hopper of the tampon dispenser in the women's lavatory.

Case 3: Our own personal experience. A distribution and service company was facing an insolvency proceeding with the potential of having a court-appointed receiver assume control of the business. The day before the court hearing, the CEO was absent from an important meeting with the company's attorneys. A thorough search found the CEO in the company cafeteria accusing the vending machine operator of shortchanging the company on its cut of three soda machines.

If you detect abuse, then your first priority is to correct the problem that permitted the abuse to occur. Maybe next year you will have time to punish the abusers, but not today and probably not this year.

by good security, and lack of appreciation can be corrected by the example of management and good communication.

To correct the problem of lack of appreciation, management must communicate with the employees the objective of the company in providing the subsidized or discounted service, the costs of providing it, and the benefits received. The company can distribute memos or post signs detailing the objectives, the costs, and the benefits. If the employees don't appreciate the value they are receiving, it's usually because management has not set the proper example to follow.

The previous brief list of common invisible benefits includes health care facilities, company nurses, and company physicians as subsidized services. These are all good benefits to provide to your employees, if the company can afford them. For some companies, these health benefits can reduce the number of sick days and lower health insurance costs. The problem with these benefits is that employees often fail to appreciate the value they are receiving. If the benefits are not resulting in costs savings and the employees are not appreciative, then the company should consider eliminating the benefits and saving the expense.

Benefits such as subsidized food services (cafeterias and kitchens), coffee and snacks, and vending machines are provided to employees and are sometimes appreciated and sometimes abused. Subsidized food services can be expensive to maintain and if not appreciated should be eliminated.

Company-provided discounts for travel (airline, automobile rental, and hotel), for shopping at stores, and for entrance to museums can be of real value to employees. Ask the vendors to let you know how much use was made of these discounts and the value that the employees received. Don't be shy! Let the employees know what a benevolent employer you are and the value they receive from the company's discounts.

Conclusions about Invisible Benefits

Be careful not to underestimate the magnitude of invisible benefits or the costs to the company. These benefits are very expen-

Exhibit 9-4. Management of invisible benefits.

Invisible Benefits

Are typically:	But with proper management:
Valuable to the employee	Values can be communicated.
Unappreciated by employees	Attitudes can be corrected by example.
Easily abused	Auditing can control abuse.
Very costly to the company	Costs can be limited and reduced.

sive and can make the difference between a profit and a loss. (See Exhibit 9-4.)

Exploring Alternatives to Layoffs

A recent survey of 836 U.S.-based companies on workforce reductions reveals that 46 percent of companies had reduced their staffing levels during the previous four years. Almost half the respondents used alternative strategies to reduce costs before resorting to firing employees.* Exhibit 9-5 illustrates the types of strategies utilized and the percentage of companies that used them.[11]

In addition, 62 percent of the companies surveyed had implemented a freeze on new hiring. While a hiring freeze can initially control the need to terminate employees, it also constricts the flow of new employees and new ideas. A company with a freeze in effect for long periods may be inhibiting its future ability to grow and remain competitive.

*The contemporary human resources euphemism for firing employees is "involuntary termination." Although the term is commonly used, it reminds us of murder. It sounds like Ian Fleming's James Bond 007 dialogue about an assassination in which the act is called a "termination with extreme prejudice."

Exhibit 9-5. Alternative strategies for preventing layoffs.

Methods for Preventing Layoffs	Percentage Using
Mandatory short workweek/workday	15%
Salary reductions or freezes	35
Demotion/downgrades/transfers to other jobs	44
Early retirement incentives	34
Voluntary separation plans	29
Voluntary job sharing	15
Limited duration furloughs	14

Reduction in the Workweek

For many years Fortune 100 companies have reduced the number of hours worked each week as an alternative to employee layoffs to reduce payroll costs. Most small and midsize companies, for an unknown reason, do not try reduced workweeks as an alternative employment strategy.

Reducing the workweek is usually most effective when a company is experiencing a slowdown in business but wants to stay poised for future growth. Consider the savings: Weekly payroll costs could be reduced by 20 percent for each day saved.

Companies can temporarily reduce the workweek by moving to a three- or four-day week or by reducing the total number of hours worked each week. When reducing the workweek, there is no assurance that employees will stay with the company. However, with the alternative being employee terminations, most staff members may agree to stay and those who leave do so voluntarily.

Large companies that have successfully implemented reduced workweeks to lower costs include General Motors, Boeing, France's electronic giant Thomson, and Data Switch.

GM. Although domestically GM prefers to use layoffs and temporary plant closings to reduce costs, in Europe it has used reduced workweeks to achieve similar objectives. In January 1993, a GM subsidiary in Germany reduced the workweek (call-

ing it short-time) to four-day weeks for a period of three months
to reduce payroll costs.

Boeing. Boeing Company, the airplane manufacturer, which
was planning on reducing its workforce by more than 20,000
personnel, is experimenting with several forms of reduced workweeks as alternatives to layoffs.

Thomson. Workers at Thomson Electronic's main plant, outside of Paris, recently agreed to a reduced workweek as an alternative to company forecasted massive layoffs. The employees
agreed to accept a forty-five-minute-per-week reduction, totaling
five fewer working days per year. The annual savings to the
company are estimated at 2 percent of total payroll costs.

Data Switch. In 1993, Data Switch Corporation, faced with a
downturn in sales of its computer products, took advantage of
an innovative program in the state of Connecticut that allows
employees to work reduced hours and be compensated by unemployment insurance for 70 percent of their pay for the remaining hours.

Where payroll represents the lion's share of overhead cost,
a reduced workweek may be a preferable alternative to layoffs.

Not all companies that consider reduced workweeks decide
to implement them as alternatives to forced terminations. The
problem of implementing a strategy of reduced workweeks is
that it distributes the effect of cost savings over the entire workforce. Some companies have opted to insulate their best workers
from these policies and prefer to lay off their less valuable employees.

In September 1992, Software Publishing Corporation, faced
with declining sales and increased competition, had to reduce
costs. According to the *San Francisco Chronicle*, the company's
senior management was very reluctant to implement layoffs and
considered several alternatives including waiting for natural at-
trition to reduce staffing and changing to a (reduced) four-day
workweek. After careful analysis, the company decided to lay
off 120 employees instead of reducing the workweek, because
according to the CEO, management had reached the conclusion

that the layoffs would "cause the least amount of pain with the maximum corporate gain."[12]

Salary Reductions or Freezes

Some companies have opted to reduce salaries in particular jobs or across the entire company as a method of reducing payroll while avoiding terminating employees. Hewlett-Packard (HP), the computer giant, until the 1990s had a strong philosophy against layoffs. In the early 1970s, HP's management recognized the need to reduce its workforce by 10 percent to meet its drop in sales. Instead of laying off 10 percent of the staff, the entire company took a mandatory 10 percent reduction in pay. HP's management believed that by equally distributing the costs of the recession it would avoid the damage to a company's culture associated with layoffs.

HP's example has been followed by other technology companies seeking to reduce costs without losing productivity in a highly competitive marketplace. To avoid layoffs, Intel Corporation reduced salaries in 1983 by 10 percent, and in 1988, Hitachi reduced all management salaries by 5 to 10 percent.

Not all management gurus agree with the technique of reducing salaries to avoid layoffs and argue that the trimming and pruning of employees (i.e., layoffs) to meet changing market conditions is necessary for the health of a company. But supporters of these alternatives believe that by equally sharing the burden during hard times, companies can avoid the negative effects of layoffs, build loyalty, and maintain the corporate culture.

Reutilization of Employees

Where employment opportunities exist for employees about to be laid off, they should be offered swiftly and with respect. Even if the job is for less pay or lower status than the previous position, the company should allow the employee the chance to accept or reject the job. No man or woman will be humbled by accepting work as an alternative to unemployment to support his or her family.

• *Demotion or transfer.* As an alternative to termination, the company can offer the employee an open position elsewhere in the organization. Don't be afraid to offer a manager a staff position or a New York–based employee a position in Chicago. Employees are greatful that the company is trying to provide for them even if the position is not the same status they were accustomed to.

• *Lending employees.* An alternative to using the employee within the company is to place the employee with a customer or vendor on a temporary basis. This has been successfully done with technicians and customer service and training personnel, who can be lent or "rented" to customers or vendors for extended periods. In this way, the employee does not lose her seniority or benefits status and the company does not necessarily lose the loyalty of the worker. There is a risk that the employee will decide not to return, but it is still a better alternative than forced unemployment.

Any employees whom you want to use in other areas of the company or transfer to other offices should be informed immediately that a position is available and told that they have only a few days to make a decision. If you allow them too much time to decide, you might lose the opportunity to make the same offer to another qualified employee.

General Motors, not usually the company to employ innovative personnel management practices, recently began pushing a new plan for finding jobs for workers laid off by GM with their suppliers. The program is called the strategic insourcing initiative. Under the program, suppliers can use GM facilities as an incentive to hire laid-off GM employees and use laid-off GM employees for temporary help. By early 1994, GM had six insourcing agreements with suppliers.

Early Retirement and Voluntary Separation

Many companies that are reluctant to lay off staff for fear of upsetting the corporate culture have offered early retirement to their employees. Early retirement programs, called voluntary separation packages, can be combined with outplacement assistance to find the retirees new employment. Although many troubled companies can barely afford payroll and cannot afford the costs of severance for a voluntary separation program, for those with deep enough pockets, it is an alternative to mandatory layoffs.

To avoid its first ever layoff, Digital Equipment Corporation during 1989 and 1990 offered a voluntary separation (retirement) benefits package to any employee who was at least fifty years old with at least five years of service. Benefits included severance pay ranging from thirteen weeks (for five years of service) to seventy-seven weeks (for twenty years), outplacement assistance, and health insurance. More than 5,500 employees took the voluntary separation package. Industry sources say these voluntary departures contributed to cost savings that allowed Digital to avoid making its first layoffs until 1991. (That year, when Digital was finally forced to make layoffs, all of the 6,900 employees laid off received the same severance package they had been offered previously for voluntary separation.)

Some companies that introduced early retirement packages were surprised by the volume of response. Dupont, which originally expected 6,500 employees to accept its plan, was surprised when more than twice that number volunteered. Unfortunately for Dupont, the company lost some employees it wanted to keep.

The problem of valuable employees accepting early retirement can be avoided by management attention to preparing employees for the coming changes. Management can use subtle persuasion to induce employees to stay or to leave and to fine-tune the technique to achieve its objectives.

Voluntary Job Sharing

Job sharing is where two employees divide the work, the pay, and the benefits of one job between themselves. Although not commonly used, job sharing has recently become more popular and was an alternative used by 15 percent of the respondents in a recent survey of companies that laid off employees. Job sharing can be an attractive alternative employment strategy in the ten states (including New York and California) that permit employees working part-time as part of a job-sharing program to receive additional subsidies in the form of partial unemployment benefits.

One prime example of a successful job-sharing program is Polaroid Corporation's. Polaroid has designed jobs so that employees alternate on either half-day or every-other-day schedules. Although most of Polaroid's job sharers are hourly factory workers, the approach could work for more senior employees. Other companies promoting job sharing as an alternative to layoffs are Bell South, Boeing, and General Motors.

Limited Duration Furloughs

Temporary layoffs, or furloughs, can include forced vacations or unpaid leaves of absence. Companies that have recently used unpaid leaves of absence to reduce costs include Polaroid, Pacific Northwest Bell, Amdahl, and Hewlett-Packard.

Where the variable costs of operating are high and would immediately be reduced by a temporary closing of facilities, the option of closing the company and temporarily furloughing all employees should be explored. This technique has primarily been used by large industrial companies, but small and medium-size businesses may also find value in closing offices and facilities for several weeks during holidays or slow seasons.

Companies that use temporary closings to furlough staff during periods of business slowdowns include the major airlines, auto manufacturers, and aircraft manufacturers.

Terminating Employees

Where redundancy is present or employees can be readily replaced, companies may choose to lay off portions of their staff.

> *Warning:* The emotional cost of firing employees can be significant. But it is better to reduce a company's costs by laying off 20 percent of employees and remaining healthy

than to be forced out of business and put 100 percent of the employees out of work.

Much as a company would like to avoid it, it is sometimes necessary. One business author has said, "Firing is one of the crucibles that turn entrepreneurs into managers, because it brings you face-to-face with failure. Nothing will make firing any easier. It shouldn't get easier. What it should become is less frequent."[13]

Before making any decisions to lay off employees, first examine methods for reducing costs and increasing revenues. Changes in costs and revenues may result in your making different choices on which employees to lay off.

It's a Dirty Job, but Someone Has to Do It

As a manager do not avoid your responsibilities when it becomes necessary to discharge employees. Don't confuse your sympathy for the employees with the necessity of sound business judgment. A profitable business that only requires fifty employees is troubled and may be unprofitable supporting a payroll of sixty.

Leon Levy, principal at Odyssey Partners, a founder of Oppenheimer & Company, and a sage among traders on Wall Street, related the story of the first employee he had to fire at Oppenheimer. The employee was courteous, likable, and hardworking, but he had been trying to do a job he was not qualified for. After several weeks, it became apparent that the employee had to be fired. Levy said he spent a day or two deliberating about how to tell the employee the news. Finally, he went to his partner, Jack Nash, and asked him to fire the employee.

Later that day, Nash fired the employee, who appeared relieved rather than grief-stricken and embraced his executioner, thanking him profusely for the opportunity and for releasing him from the job. The employee said he knew management was unsatisfied with him but that he felt too much loyalty to quit.

I don't know if the story is apocryphal or true, but Levy's observations are still worth repeating. First, avoid delays after you have made the decision to fire an employee. Second, if someone isn't able to perform the responsibilities of the job, then you aren't doing him a favor by retaining him.

Once the decision has been made to terminate an employee, there are some basic rules we can offer the manager charged with the responsibility of informing the subordinate. These rules give you a script to follow and help to make the process efficient and expeditious.

The standard rules of good management apply when terminating employees. As mentioned before, don't model your behavior upon Arnold Schwarzenegger's portrayal of a futuristic hit man in *The Terminator*, but on the other extreme, don't imitate Jimmy Stewart in *It's a Wonderful Life*. A good manager should be effective and compassionate yet remain firm when executing sound business decisions.

When to Schedule the Termination Meeting

Don't wait until weeks after the decision has been made to inform the employee. Bad news travels fast, and waiting even a few days may be enough time for the employee to have heard through the grapevine instead of hearing it from you. The meeting should be held as soon as possible after the decision.

Try to choose a day for the meeting toward the later part of the week. This way if there is any internal fallout, it won't interfere with the majority of the week and after a weekend has elapsed, the effect will be further pacified.

Choose a time after lunch. People are more relaxed after eating, and if they react with strong emotions to the news, they can leave the office early without losing face or disturbing the work flow.

What You Need to Be Prepared

When meeting with an employee to inform him of his imminent termination, you should be prepared with four documents that will provide you with a script to follow during the meeting. These documents should be contained in a closed folder to be presented to the employee at the conclusion of your meeting. Retain a duplicate copy of each document for your own records.

The documents are: (1) a formal signed letter of termination, (2) a statement of accrued and termination benefits, (3) a copy of the company policy regarding termination, and (4) a letter of recommendation.

The Letter of Termination

A termination letter is a very succinct one-paragraph document. The letter is addressed to the employee informing him that he has been terminated with a clear statement of the reasons and the effective date.

In the case of a troubled business, the letter should state that the employee was terminated because the company's business has declined (or the division is being closed, the work is being transferred to another location, etc.), and therefore the individual's services are no longer required.

The letter should briefly thank the employee for his years of service and inform him that he can discuss his termination benefits with the personnel department (or whoever is the designated benefits contact person).

The Statement of Benefits

The employee's statement of accrued and termination benefits should detail all salary, commissions, vacation pay, paid sick leave, and expense reimbursement owed to the employee as of the effective date of termination. The statement should also include any termination benefits that the employee is eligible for, such as COBRA insurance conversion rights, retirement and pension plan rights, and severance pay. (COBRA is the acronym for the Consolidated Omnibus Budget Reconciliation Act. This act contains the federal laws governing an employee's rights to continue his insurance coverage after termination of employment.)

Be certain that the statement includes debits for monies the employee owes to the company, including cash advances, loans, or payment for vacation or sick leave taken before being earned.

If the employee has equipment in his personal possession such as a computer, a fax machine, a cellular telephone, or a pager, then this equipment should be detailed in the statement along with a note that the final check will not be given to the employee until the equipment listed has been returned to the company. Equipment is an asset of the company and while in the possession of the employee is a liability that the employee owes to the company.

If the termination is effective on the same day or the next day and the employee has no outstanding liabilities to the company, then it is good form at the meeting to present the employee with a check for the full amount owed to him (except for severance benefits).

The Company Policy Regarding Termination

If the company has an employee handbook or a policy manual that details its policy toward terminated employees, include a copy of the policy along with the statement of benefits. This will avoid any confusion that may arise. Employees often confuse what they have "heard" about termination benefits with the official policy of the company.

The Letter of Recommendation

All employees, except those terminated for gross incompetence or criminal activity or those who worked for the company for less than three months, deserve a letter of recommendation to use when looking for future employment. A letter of recommendation will lessen the traumatic effects of the firing to the employee and will serve as good public relations to the surviving employees that they will be treated well when they leave. You also want to avoid the so-called grudge factor, the resentment that employees feel when one of their colleagues is fired. These grudges can affect morale and reduce productivity.

A letter of recommendation also increases the efficiency of the termination process because it avoids the necessity of the employee coming back to ask for a letter next week, next month, or next year.

Keep the letter to less than one page. Detail the length of the employee's tenure with the company, the initial and final positions held, and the types of work he was responsible for. Do not put any negative comments into the letter. Your writing should accent the employee's strengths, hard work, attitude, and commitment. The letter should be addressed to whom it may concern and be signed by the most senior person in the company who had knowledge of the employee's performance.

The letter should not discuss the reasons for the discharge. Your statement that you would recommend the individual for another position is the primary purpose of this letter, not the reasons leading up to his departure.

Step-by-Step Guide to Terminating Employees

1. Schedule the meeting as soon as possible after the decision has been made. Try for a time toward the end of the week, preferably after lunch. Do not give the employee advance warning of what is to be discussed at the meeting.

Some managers prefer to conduct the meeting in surroundings that are familiar to the employee. You may want to meet with the employee in his office or in a private conference room near his desk or work area.

2. In advance, inform the person responsible for benefits and have her generate the statement of accrued and termination benefits for presentation to the employee.

Have the statement double-checked. If you have reason to believe that the employee will question or disagree with the statement, then attach a copy of the supporting documentation.

3. Be prepared for your meeting. Have your documents ready:

- A formal signed letter of termination
- A statement of accrued and termination benefits
- A copy of the company policy regarding termination
- A letter of recommendation

4. Be serious about your role. Be yourself, but be formal. Make certain that you will not be disturbed by interruptions dur-

ing the meeting. Begin the meeting by informing the employee that because of the economic pressures facing the company, it is no longer possible to retain his valued services and that he is being terminated as of the effective date.

5. Thank the employee for his years of service and hard work. Open the folder containing the four documents and tell him that the folder is for him and that it contains a letter of termination and a letter of recommendation to assist him in obtaining a new position.

Don't give him the folder until the meeting ends. He will have plenty of time to read the enclosures after the meeting.

6. Inform the employee that he is entitled to certain accrued and termination benefits that are detailed in the benefits statement also enclosed in the folder and that he can discuss the details with the designated benefits person in the company. Tell him that also enclosed in the folder, for his reference, is a copy of the company's policy on terminated employees.

7. Advise the employee that you expect him to perform the responsibilities of his position in a professional manner during his remaining tenure.

Wish him well and then stand up, shake his hand, and either show him to the door or, if you are in his office, leave the room. Don't linger in the area and chat with other employees. Let the discharged employee inform his colleagues himself.

8. Most important, keep the meeting brief. There is nothing you can tell the employee that isn't contained in the folder you are presenting him with and little you can do for him unless you have an outplacement program.

The longer you and the employee sit together, the more likely he is to become emotional. You are not being insensitive by leaving. Being fired is indeed an emotional experience, but not one that you as a manager should be sharing with your employee.

Outplacement

Laying off employees is never easy, though if the employee is qualified you can make the process easier for her—as well as earn considerable goodwill in your company and present a positive public image—by providing formalized or personal outplacement services.

Outplacement is assisting an employee to obtain a new position. You can do this simply by making telephone calls to your personal or business contacts. There are also employment search groups and agencies that specialize in outplacement and assist companies in trying to place employees whose services are no longer required.

The last few years has seen the emergence of specialized outplacement consulting firms to provide these services.* Some cities and states also provide outplacement assistance to companies that will be laying off large numbers of employees. Proactive companies have even taken out advertisements in newspapers and trade journals soliciting potential employers to call special hotlines, voluntarily staffed by the employees, to hire laid-off employees.

Hewlett-Packard, known for its innovative personnel policies, recently germinated two small businesses to provide jobs for employees from departments that were going to be reduced or terminated. The departments provided internal training and technical writing services to the company. The departing employees accepted reduced salaries and benefits but did not have to face the prospect of unemployment.

Research among fired managers shows that many would rather have more cash in their severance packages as an option/alternative to the services of an outplacement agency. The cost of these agencies can be up to $20,000 per manager, versus $5,000 cash to workers as an alternative.

---

*Many companies now provide outplacement assistance as part of their severance package for laid-off employees. Large companies that recently provided these services include Eckerd Drugs, Lockheed, Macy's, General Electric, Boeing, General Motors, and Safeway. However, outplacement is no longer limited to just large companies. Small and midsize companies and even nonprofits are turning more toward the use of specialized outplacement companies as a more humane way of taking care of discharged employees. The outplacement consulting business, which was in its infancy in the early 1980s, was estimated to have 1992 annual gross revenues of $600 million.

Notes

1. See Robert M. Tomasko, *Downsizing: Reshaping the Corporation for the Future*, 2d ed. (New York: AMACOM, 1989) for an excellent look at streamlining companies for future growth and competitiveness. The book explores the risks of layoffs to achieve cost reductions and alternative strategies that companies should consider.

2. Joanne Chianello, "400 Firms to Cut Staff to Aid Profit," *Financial Post* (Toronto), April 14, 1993, p. 6, quoting a study of 505 companies on layoffs and profitability by the outplacement consulting firm Right Associates; Jeff Pelline and Kenneth Howe, "Downsizing Corporate America: Cost-Cutting Trend Sparks a Workplace Revolution, *San Francisco Chronicle*, October 26, 1992, p. B1, quoting an American Management Association survey of 836 U.S.-based companies on workforce reductions that occurred between July 1991 and July 1992.

3. Brian S. Moskal, "Managing Survivors," *Industry Week*, August 3, 1992, p. 14.

4. Pelline and Howe.

5. Susan Feyder, "Regis Corp. Drops Health Insurance for its Employees: Blames Ridiculous Costs," *Star Tribune* (Kansas City), March 5, 1992, p. D1.

6. Tony Bartlett, "Hawaiian Air to Suspend Services, Beef Up Others," *Travel Weekly*, November 30, 1992, p. 48.

7. "Firm's Gamble Paid Off: Metro Bolt Buys New Quarters," *Crains Detroit Business*, September 14, 1992, p. 3.

8. James Bennet, "$10 Billion for G.M. Pensions," *New York Times*, May 12, 1994, p. D-1.

9. "Pension Plan Underfunding Will Exceed $50 Billion for 1992, Slate Tells Council," *BNA Pension & Benefits Reporter*, Dec. 13, 1993, vol. 20, no. 49, p. 2571.

10. *Retiree Health Benefits: An Era of Uncertainty* (Newark, N.J.: KPMG Peat Marwick, 1993).

11. Chianello; Pelline and Howe.

12. Pelline and Howe.

13. Karen E. Carney, "How to Fire," *Inc.*, May 1992, p. 67.

10

Selling Your
Business

When creditors are knocking at your door and there is no money to pay the bills, do not despair. Although your company is in distress, you may still be able to sell it or get someone to invest in it. You may think the business is worthless; however, your misfortune may be a timely opportunity for someone else.

The blood, sweat, and tears invested in starting a business are often worth more to a potential buyer or investor than an owner of a troubled business realizes. He has a valuable property to offer: a fully equipped and operational business with an established base of customers. The company worked hard to get to where it is, but along the way, it ran into some problems. The company still has good prospects. The business is still viable; it is searching for the right partner. With good marketing and a positive attitude, a troubled business can often be sold for more than its book value.

No business, least of all a troubled one, can be sold overnight. It takes a series of steps, a process: locating and recruiting potential purchasers, building trust, performing due diligence, validating the business, confirming the financing, negotiating the price, agreeing to terms, and then consummating the sale.

Whether you are selling the entire business or parts of it, or seeking a financial investment in your business, the process is

Parts of this chapter were adapted from Matthew L. Shuchman, "Selling Points," *Entrepreneur*, July 1994.

Exhibit 10-1. Steps in selling a business.

Buyer's Role	Process Step	Seller's Role
Marketing		
• What's for sale?	• Confidentiality agreement	• Locate and recruit prospects.
• Can we afford it?	• Sales memorandum	• Qualify prospects.
Sales		
• Is the business viable?	• Building confidence	• Tell your story.
• Do we want it?	• Letter of understanding	• What do they really want?
• Is it worth looking further?	• Escrow agreement, deposit escrow	• What do we want?
Due Diligence		
• Verify financials and business.	• Provide documentation.	• Use supporting documents.
• Obtain approvals and confirm financing.	• Negotiate terms and conditions.	• Do we want this deal? Is it a good fit?
Closing		
• Purchase	• Contract	• Sale!

very similar. Exhibit 10-1 outlines the basic steps in selling a troubled business.

Marketing Your Business

The sales memorandum is the most important document in selling any business. This three-to-four-page summary answers two questions: (1) What's for sale? and (2) why would someone be interested in buying? One consultant who has been involved with many sales of troubled companies says, "To maximize its value, the owners of a troubled company should be selling not just the assets but their vision of the future and their plan for how the business can achieve it." The sales memorandum, together with certain lists (customers, inventories, etc.), legal documents (leases, contracts, loan agreements, etc.), and financial reports, should tell a convincing story about the company.

Outline for a Sales Memorandum

1. What is for sale?
   - Describe the business and list assets.
   - Discuss sales for last three years and current forecast.
   - Describe customers, staff, plant, and equipment.
2. Why is it for sale?
3. What are the sales price and terms?
4. Who are the potential purchasers?
5. What is the company's history (founding, achievements, mission statement)?
6. Who should be contacted?

1. *What is for sale?* Are you selling the entire business? Inventory? Just the customer list? Describe the business offered for sale and list the assets included. Briefly discuss the sales for last three years and your current forecast. How large is the company? Provide a thumbnail sketch of the company including the number and type of customers and staff and a list of plant and equipment.

2. *Why is it for sale?* Tell a story that a prudent businessperson would believe. Be honest and sound credible. Good reasons are the retirement or illness of the principals, the expiration of the lease, the fact that the company grew too fast, or the need for additional working capital (i.e., creditors are becoming hostile or the burden of past due taxes is crushing).

3. *What are the sales price and terms?* Don't be too detailed but let the reader know if she qualifies as a potential purchaser. Give a price range, list fixed terms and assets, and discuss the future availability of the principals. Is there a bank loan or mortgage that the new owner could assume? What is the minimum cash payment required? If you have an overdue tax payment of

$200,000, then don't be shy. Tell potential buyers that at least $200,000 of the sale price is required to be in cash. Let the buyer know the framework you want to work in. Defining price and terms clearly can avoid those "You never told me it had to be an all cash offer!" problems.

4. *Who are the potential purchasers?* Who would be interested in purchasing the company? Let the reader know if this includes a company in the same business, a complimentary business, or an entity with specific investment objectives.

5. *What is the company's history?* In one or two paragraphs bring the reader up to date from answering the question of how the company was founded to the present, including any significant achievements since its founding. Include the company's mission statement and how it relates to the company's current focus.

The following is a good example of a brief corporate history of the fictional EZ Oil Change company:

> EZ Oil Change, Inc., was founded and financed in 1986 by two former automobile mechanics to provide rapid and inexpensive oil changes for passenger cars on the North Shore of Long Island, N.Y. In 1987 it opened its first location and has opened one new location every two years since its founding. Currently, the company is enhancing each location to add tire sales and service.

6. *Who should be contacted?* Will you speak to potential purchasers, or would you prefer that your lawyer or business broker screen and qualify them first? (A well-designed screening process can save considerable time.)

Locating Potential Purchasers

Potential purchasers are easy to approach if you have a good story to tell. Start by approaching the contacts you have in everyday business.

Potential Purchasers

- Major suppliers
- Major competitors of your suppliers
- Competitors
- Businesses in related areas
- Executives from your industry
- Major creditors
- Major customers

Major Suppliers

A major vendor or supplier of your company is an ideal candidate to invest in your business. As long as you stay in business and purchase products from him, the supplier will prosper. Many suppliers are reluctant to invest in any of their customers for fear of alienating another customer, but this rule does not apply if your company has an exclusive (contractual or de facto) arrangement with the supplier for a particular market. Even if the supplier cannot directly make an investment, he may be an excellent source of leads to other potential investors.

Major Competitors of Your Suppliers

If your major supplier is not interested or is not approachable as a potential investor, then consider your supplier's competition. This is not a disloyal act; it is a question of survival!

If you currently sell one brand of personal computers and neither the manufacturer nor the distributor can assist you financially, then discretely approach the manufacturer and the distributor of competing product lines. The competitor of your supplier may have been scheming for years on how to steal you away from your current supplier and grow you as a customer. He has a very large incentive to assist you; his reward will be your future business.

Competitors

Surprisingly to many troubled companies, the most unlikely parties—your present competitors—can become your natural allies in the business of survival. By purchasing your company, your competitor can eliminate your threat as competition while securing your relationship as a friendly colleague.

The first objective in this process is to identify your competitors properly. Who are they? Make a list of your current competitors.

More than one business owner has told us that they didn't have any competitors. They admitted there were other companies in similar businesses but insisted that these companies couldn't provide the same quality of service. Saying that you don't have any competitors is a falsehood and a myth to hide behind.

With very few exceptions, all businesses have competitors. You may not perceive that they provide the products and services in the same way as your company, but they are still your competition. Don't let your ego or your image of the company interfere with your judgment of who your competitors are.

Ask yourself the question: If you were to shut your doors tomorrow, who would your customers turn to as a replacement for your company?

Then assemble a brief dossier on each of your competitors. This dossier should include: company name, addresses, names of principals and senior managers, telephone and fax numbers, number of employees, breakdown of staff (management, professional, support, etc.), estimated annual sales, type of ownership (public, private), major customers, authorized dealerships or specialties, and current business profile.

If you don't know your competitors personally, don't wait any longer; seek them out. Don't let your ego get in your way. You don't need an intermediary. They probably know who you are, so they are likely to return your telephone call. Meet them now. Have a drink with them. Don't wait until the last moment; you may lose valuable opportunities in the interim. (See Exhibit 10-2 for reasons why you should know your competitors.)

Warning: Be very guarded in your approaches to your competitors. They are in a strategic position to exploit the information you reveal to them about your precarious financial condition.

Exhibit 10-2. Why it is important to know your competition.

The company's competitors are valuable for many reasons: (1) as joint venture partners, (2) as customers for excess inventory, (3) as potential destinations for the outplacement of employees, and (4) as potential buyers for the business.

1. Competitors can be helpful in situations where your company is no longer able to operate independently. These joint ventures may be a business opportunity that is outside of your regional service area or a project that is too big for your company.
2. Should you have excess inventory of spare parts, new merchandise, or used equipment, your prime customers for the excess inventory could be your competition.
3. If you need to lay off employees because you are terminating a division, there is no harm in contacting your competitors, who could utilize your loyal employees.
4. If you decide to sell all or part of your business, your competitor is an ideal candidate to be a potential purchaser.

The discussion at the first meeting with a competitor should concentrate on the strengths of a "union" between the companies, the ability to devote the combined efforts at obtaining new business, the power of the combined resources, and the synergy of all the excellent talent available to the potential union. Don't go too heavily into a discussion of your company's immediate financial needs. Describe your company's needs for additional working capital to grow to the next stage to achieve dreams that both you and your competitor share.

If there is strong interest from a competitor in a potential union, then seek legal counsel and protection immediately.

Protect Your Company

First and foremost, your competitor must execute a confidentiality, nondisclosure, and noncircumvention agreement. The document should state clearly that the only reason for exchanging information with your competitor is the furtherance of ventures that profit both parties.

Second, if you are selling any inventory, fixed assets, or spare parts to your competitor, make certain the payment terms are cash, COD, or certified check. Particularly if you have creditors, the sale of assets, though not intended to defraud your creditors, could raise some eyebrows with a nasty creditor, or an unscrupulous competitor could cause the payments to be frozen or redirected away from your company at a critical time.

Many is the company that considered purchasing a troubled colleague in another region and failed to consummate the transaction. Within a year, it had established operations in direct competition having learned the recipe for success during the prior due diligence period. Though the troubled company can respond with litigation, it has already suffered the damage.

The lesson to be learned is that legal protection is a requirement, but there is no substitute for carefully evaluating a potential purchaser and her motivation. If the potential purchaser believes she can achieve the same strategic or financial objectives without acquiring your company, she probably will.

Businesses in Related Areas

Businesses in related areas are potential competitors, but for reasons of geography or market specialization, they do not directly compete with you in your marketplace. They may be dealers of the same or similar product lines located in another major city, businesses that sell the same services as your company but only to residential customers while you sell exclusively to commercial customers, or businesses that sell the same products exclusively by mail order that you sell directly.

David Farber is CFO of New Jersey–based Garden State Business Machines, which is growing by acquiring underperforming businesses in the same as well as other geographic markets. He believes your colleagues should be high on the list of potential purchasers to contact. He says, "Focus on contacting companies in the same or similar business that don't compete in your marketplace. These strategic buyers are more likely to see the underlying value in your troubled business because they understand it and know what is required to fix it."

Executives from Your Industry

These executives can be a valuable and knowledgeable talent pool and may provide the added confidence necessary to attract investors.

Major Creditors

Unless you are a very large company or your creditor is also a supplier, major creditors are unlikely to be interested in being investors. You should still approach them as they may have leads to pursue potential investors.

> *Warning:* When your business is close to insolvency, do not reveal this information to a major creditor unless the revelation is part of a renegotiation strategy. Creditors with knowledge of your pending insolvency will act to protect their own interests. The acts of a major creditor with knowledge of your insolvency can include refusing to provide additional financing, freezing of bank accounts, and refusing to be flexible with payment terms. In the most severe cases, a creditor can initiate insolvency proceedings that can lead to a court-appointed receivership or an involuntary bankruptcy filing.

Major Customers

Don't ignore your major customers as potential investors. Your customers know your story; they know the service that you can deliver and your commitment to the business. The question your customers will ask is, "Why?" and assuming they can understand your story, they will need to decide if the investment is prudent for them. Don't be too afraid to reveal the way you do business to your customers. They are aware that you need to make a profit to survive.

> *Warning:* Do not reveal so much information to your cus-
> tomers that they will fear for your continued survival, and
> don't approach them unless you have a strong and secure
> relationship with them. Dissatisfied customers with knowl-
> edge of your business can hurt you even more than com-
> petitors.

Using Business Brokers

If you are unable to locate qualified candidates or need to shield
your identity, then don't hesitate to involve a business broker or
independent third party early in the marketing process. Experiences with business brokers vary, but it is important to find one
who understands your business. Stephen Hopkins, president of
Nightingale Associates, a turnaround consulting company located in New Canaan, Connecticut, says, "Typical business brokers don't know your business and you may do better with an
informed third party, like your accountant or lawyer, who understands your company."

Considering Investment Banks

You may also want to consider the traditional investors in privately owned companies: venture capital funds and investment
groups. These financial players will be interested only if your
company is large enough in your industry to be significant;
owns valuable rights, franchises, or patents; or is developing a
new technology that could revolutionize your industry.

Investment firms can also be a valuable source for leads to
potential buyers and may broker the sale for a commission.
These firms are experienced at buying and selling businesses
and can also provide a critical review of your sales memorandum.

Sales Process

Once you have located qualified prospects, work closely with
them to convince them that the business is viable, that they

vince the buyer that the business is solid, your employees are hardworking, and your customers are loyal. Never, never, never stop selling. Sell hard and be honest—but don't oversell as you will get caught by your boasts and exaggerations. *Building trust is the key element to the successful sale of a troubled business.* Don't tell the potential buyer that revenues will double in the next year. He won't believe you and it will place your entire credibility at issue. Give the buyer a story he can go home and tell his spouse about that makes sense.

Let the Seller Beware: Evaluating Potential Investors and Purchasers

Common practice is to regard due diligence as only about the seller. This is wrong. Particularly if the sale involves payments over time or the assumption of obligations, you need to know more about the buyer. Spending a morning in the local courthouse can answer many questions about a purchaser, including a history of prior litigation, property filings, and tax liens.

There are many elements involved in evaluating potential investors and purchasers. The types of questions that you would ask of a competitor wanting to increase his market share are not the same as those you would ask of an individual with a $10 million inheritance who wants to purchase a business. Below are detailed the more important questions to consider when evaluating potential buyers.

Questions for Evaluating Buyers

- Can they afford it?
- How will they finance it (cash, loan, mortgage, or leverage)?
- Why are they investing (strategic or financial)?
- Do they need bank, Small Business Administration, or other approvals?
- What do they want (assets, franchise, customers, employees)?
- How quickly can they close?

Can They Afford It?

The first question you need to answer about any potential buyer is whether she can afford the price, i.e., is it worth your while to continue a dialogue with her?

Unfortunately, it can sometimes take several meetings to determine exactly what is being purchased and what the price is. To avoid wasting time with candidates who cannot afford the investment, early in the process—usually at the end of the first meeting—don't be shy and ask the candidate how she intends to finance the investment. Tell her that you are very interested in going forward but that you need some proof that she has adequate financial backing, at least within the range necessary to consummate a transaction.

How Will They Finance It?

Many a seller has been surprised when at the end of the due diligence period unforeseen delays or new terms and conditions appear as dictated by a "lender," and the buyer informs the seller that the transaction is still subject to the buyer receiving adequate financing. If the transaction involves a loan or a mortgage on existing real estate or property, or property to be acquired, then verify that the buyer has approval or at least determine how long the process will take.

If the deal is for all cash, then ask for some proof that the investor has the magnitude of cash available to him for this type of transaction.

The types of financing to be most careful about, for the seller, are those where the buyer intends to leverage (borrow against) your company's assets or future cash flow to pay for the business. Although this is commonly done with larger LBO (leveraged buy out) transactions, with smaller and medium-size businesses, the transaction can get very sticky with a payment schedule that stretches over some time period.

Should a payment schedule over time be part of the payment terms, then you need to perform due diligence carefully upon the purchaser because you are relying on his assets and good business judgment to secure your future payment stream.

Why Are They Investing?

Investors can be divided into two categories based on the reason they are making the investment.

1. *Strategic* players are those who are already in the business or a related business, or who desire to enter your marketplace and are making the investment for particular business reasons not all of which are financial. Strategic players are usually patient and are willing to build or rebuild a business in the short run for a financial return in the longer term.
2. *Financial* players are interested strictly in receiving an economic return on their investment in some limited period of time. The period of time for their investment can be from a few months to a few years, but it is generally not a long-term investment unless your company has plans for making a public stock offering.

Warning: Be wary of wolves dressed in sheeps' clothing. Financial players may approach you dressed as strategic investors, and strategic investors may tell you their only interest is a financial return. Both of these actors can cause you to play your role incorrectly and to ask the wrong questions. Examining a potential investor's past track record is a reasonably good predictor of his future performance.

Do They Need Bank, SBA, or Other Approvals?

Don't wait until a few days before closing to discover that your potential buyer needs to have the investment approved by his board of directors, his bank, or his franchiser before he can proceed. In some industries, regulatory approval, even pro forma, may be required. Investigate early what approvals will be required on the buyer's side; you already know what approvals are necessary on the seller's side.

What Do They Want?

This question should more aptly be put as: What do they *really* want? If this is a strategic investment, then the investor may really be interested not in your company but in one or more of your selected assets. These objects of desire can include your real estate, your franchise rights, your exclusive on a particular territory or marketplace, your regulatory license to operate, your customer base, your employees, or your managers.

> *Warning:* Once you have determined what assets you possess that are of strategic importance to the potential investor, guard them dearly. If the investor is most interested in your senior management, be prepared that, if the plans for investment fail, he will try to acquire members of your senior management team without acquiring your company.

How Quickly Can They Close?

How quickly do *you* need to close? Do you have six months (not likely if you are reading this book), thirty days, sixty days, or ninety days? Don't sound desperate, but if you absolutely must have a commitment and a closed deal (i.e., check in hand) within the following thirty days, then tell the potential investor.

Moving to a Commitment

Most investors are either in a rush, saying, "Only have today and tomorrow to examine the deal," or they are interested but say, "We won't be able to get back to you for six weeks." As the seller you need to control the process. Tell the buyer when you expect a commitment and when you need to close. If she is interested, she'll find a way to accommodate your needs, and if not, then as a troubled business, you shouldn't be talking to her. Many engagements fall apart before reaching the altar. Last-minute jitters are more common in a business union than in a marriage. The key to a successful sale is to maintain good communications with your suitors. Talk to them regularly.

Most important, *do not let outside advisors push the process into a breakup.* Lawyers are notorious for making ultimatums and setting absolute conditions and causing otherwise eligible and compatible suitors to become adversaries.

Types of Sales

The type of sale that can be arranged is dependent upon the financial condition of the buyer and the seller, the assets that are being sold, the condition of the assets (i.e., whether they are being used as security for financial obligations), and the need for the principals to remain involved with the business.

Can You Sell the Corporation?

The simplest though riskiest transaction is the sale of the company's shares. By purchasing the corporation, a buyer inherits all of its obligations, debts, and history. With troubled businesses these liabilities can include past due taxes, penalties, pending litigation, accounts payable, leasing obligations, and employee benefits. If these liabilities are significant or unknown, the buyer may still be interested in the business but not the corporation. Selling the business without the corporation is called a bulk asset sale (discussed below).

Although some assets can be obtained without purchasing the corporation, many may not be separable or transferrable. If the business has assets such as franchise rights, service contracts, employment agreements, patents, favorable leases, or real estate, then it may be necessary to sell the corporation and all that goes along with the legal entity. *Seek professional advice on selling the corporation versus selling only selected assets.*

What about Bulk Asset Sales?

State laws governing debtor and creditor relations vary, but disposing of significant assets beyond what would be considered ordinary business is generally prohibited unless public notice is given to your creditors. Although these statutes were enacted to prevent a business from selling major assets without concern for its creditors, this doesn't mean you are required to telephone each of your creditors and remind them you have found a buyer.

In 1990, Erin Data Systems of Happague, Long Island, New York, a troubled computer products distributor, finally ran out of working capital. With millions of dollars owed to creditors around the country, it arranged a bulk asset sale of its inventory and customer list to JWP, Inc., a better capitalized competitor. The sale was completed and the Erin owners received funds that permitted them to negotiate settlements with their creditors. Two weeks later, a California-based company that was owed $400,000 protested the sale, but it was too late. *Don't be surprised if you are more conscious of the company's debts than your creditors.*

What about Sales from Bankruptcy?

A company that has filed for bankruptcy can still be sold. Don't file for bankruptcy to make it easier to sell the company, but neither should you give up hope of selling after filing. More than one company has discovered that after filing, a bidding war developed that raised the sale price. Sales from bankruptcy are a special art and should be handled only by an experienced attorney.

What Happens to Your Employees?

It is difficult to guarantee jobs for all of your employees after your company is sold. Don't make promises that you will be unable to keep. The decisions about employees will be made by the new owners, not the former owners. Let them be the bad guys.

Since President Lincoln issued the Emancipation Proclamation in 1863, it has been contrary to U.S. law to own personnel, but employees are "bought and sold" every day—they are just compensated for the privilege. Most employees don't care who owns their company; it's just a question of who their direct manager is and what their future prospects are for compensation, benefits, and career advancement. If specific employees are an integral part of your business, you may want to work with the potential purchaser to negotiate employment contracts for these employees to secure their services.

These agreements can result in win-win-win situations. The employee benefits by knowing she will receive a salary and usually a bonus; the purchaser benefits from knowing he has secured the loyal services of an important employee; and the seller benefits from having overcome one of the obstacles to consummating a sale.

Closings

Less ominous than it sounds, a closing is simply the meeting of the parties (or their designated representatives) to finalize and consummate the transaction. Any adjustments to the price, terms, and agreements are made at the closing. The easiest way to have a successful closing is to be prepared, agree in advance on the documents that need to be exchanged and executed, be certain both buyer and seller have the opportunity to review the agreements, and—most important—plan for contingencies.

Remember that it takes courage for an entrepreneur to sell his or her business. Although selling will not leave you as an independent owner, it may relieve you of the threat of economic ruin and it allows you to go forward and start your next business. The keys to a successful sale are proper planning, good marketing, and a positive attitude.

11

Bankruptcy

Warning: Even a personal or small-business bankruptcy can be a rocky road full of potential liabilities. Always seek the counsel of an experienced and competent attorney before making any decisions about bankruptcy.

Bankruptcy is the legal mechanism granted by the U.S. Constitution that allows individuals or entities to petition the bankruptcy court for relief from the burden of their debts. Bankruptcy is available to all persons and entities that reside or have a domicile, a place of business, or property in the United States.

The intent of our founding fathers in enacting the bankruptcy laws was to give a person a fresh start to continue his life without the weighty obligation of debts incurred prior to the bankruptcy. Bankruptcy also establishes equity among creditors ensuring that each creditor receives only his share of the debtor's estate. Congress has made many amendments and revisions to the original laws governing bankruptcy, the most recent major revision being the Bankruptcy Reform Act of 1978. The laws governing bankruptcy are commonly called the Bankruptcy Code.*

One philosophical view of bankruptcy is that it keeps the

*The Bankruptcy Code includes those laws contained in the Bankruptcy Reform Act of 1978, the Bankruptcy Amendments and Federal Judgeship Act of 1984, the Bankruptcy Judges, United States Trustees, and Family Farmer Act of 1986, and amendments made to the Code by subsequent sessions of Congress. Prior to Congress's enactment of the 1978 reforms, the group of federal laws that regulated bankruptcy were called the Bankruptcy Act.

debtor honest or at least gives him a conscience of a sort. As Frank Borman, Apollo astronaut and former chairman of Eastern Airlines—which went into bankruptcy while under his helm—said, "Capitalism without bankruptcy is like Christianity without hell." An alternative view was held by the actor Errol Flynn, who was perpetually in debt and said, "Any man who has $10,000 left when he dies is a failure."

Bankruptcy, in its simplest form, allows a debtor who petitions the court to be relieved of the obligation to pay all of those debts that are dischargeable under the Bankruptcy Code. The more intricate forms of bankruptcy give the debtor the opportunity to reorganize her financial affairs, propose a plan to settle with creditors, and, after obtaining the approval of creditors and the court, be granted a fresh start.

Bankruptcy professionals use terms and expressions that are as unique to their trade as the lingo of physicists describing atomic particles. When speaking with professionals about a potential bankruptcy filing, ask them to define *in plain language* any special terms or legal or Latin expressions. At the end of this chapter is a section on the special terms used in bankruptcy.

How Do You Spell Relief?

To request relief under the Bankruptcy Code, the party requesting relief (referred to as the debtor) must petition the court and submit a series of official forms describing the debtor's personal or business financial situation or both. The petition and supporting forms are filed (given to) the clerk of the bankruptcy court. The clerk stamps the documents with the date and assigns a bankruptcy case number. The debtor, having received a case number, has officially filed for bankruptcy and is granted the first form of relief, spelled "automatic stay."

The automatic stay stops creditors from continuing most actions against the debtor and her property except through recourse available to them in the bankruptcy court. Most proceedings in federal and state courts, in which the debtor is a

defendant party, are stayed (suspended) pending the outcome
of the bankruptcy proceeding.*

The automatic stay prevents creditors from foreclosing on
loans and enforcing judgments and liens and even halts the IRS,
state, and local taxing authorities from enforcing collection without the permission of the bankruptcy court. (Even creditors
holding claims that are nondischargeable in bankruptcy, such as
payroll withholding and sales taxes, are stayed from collection
efforts during the pendency of the bankruptcy. The obligation
for the nondischargeable debt survives; however, the debtor is
given some breathing space during the pendency of a bankruptcy proceeding.)

Types of Bankruptcy

There are many types of bankruptcy protection depending on
the debtor's personal financial status or condition of the business. Bankruptcy relief can be requested by the debtor (called
voluntary bankruptcy) or by the debtor's creditors (involuntary
bankruptcy). Bankruptcies are referred to by the chapter (section
or §) of the Bankruptcy Code that controls and discharges each
type of debtor.

All of the types of bankruptcy fall into two categories: liquidations and reorganizations. Chapter 13, called a debt adjustment, is a special type of reorganization available only to
individuals. Liquidations are called chapter 7 and reorganizations are called chapters 9, 11, 12, and 13. Of these, chapter 9 is
for use by municipalities and chapter 12 is limited to farmers.
The discussion in this book is limited to chapters 7, 11, and 13.

---

*Not all litigation against the debtor is stayed by a bankruptcy filing. The Bank-
ruptcy Code (11 U.S.C. § 105) limits the power of the bankruptcy court only to
act to "protect the integrity of the bankrupt's estate. . . ." Examples of litigation that are not stayed by a bankruptcy filing include most criminal proceedings, proceedings to collect alimony or child support, proceedings for issuing
bad checks, and proceedings for failure to comply with environmental laws.
See Bankruptcy Code, 11 U.S.C. § 362(b).

Liquidations

In a bankruptcy liquidation, except for personal property that is exempt, all property not already used as security for obligations is sold (i.e., liquidated) for the benefit of the creditors. Liquidations are the least expensive and the most common form of bankruptcy.

Reorganizations

A reorganization under chapter 11 is a petition to the bankruptcy court for the debtor to seek temporary relief from creditors while he proposes a plan for repaying at least some of his debt. The debtor must obtain approval from the creditors for the plan and seek confirmation from the court before reorganizing.

The plan is a proposal under which creditors would receive at least as much value in a reorganization as in a liquidation under chapter 7. Upon approval of the plan, the business is permitted either to continue operations or begin an orderly liquidation to fund the payments required under the plan. The bankruptcy code defines the necessary elements of a plan and the process for obtaining acceptance from the bankrupt's creditors and confirmation from the court. Chapter 11 filings are most commonly used by larger businesses although they are available for use by individuals. Reorganizations are the most expensive form of bankruptcy.

Requirements for Reorganization

Essential requirements for the court to confirm a plan of reorganization include the facts that: (1) the debtor has a source of income sufficient to make the payments required by the plan; (2) the plan must be viable; (3) the reorganization must be in the "best interests" of the creditors; and (4) the plan must be proposed in "good faith."

In practice, each judge and each district use other litmus tests to decide whether a debtor may be permitted to reorganize or forced to liquidate. These tests can include quantitative criteria such as requiring a plan to promise creditors payment of 15 or 20 cents for every dollar of their claims. The court may also use tests such as the relative difference between what the creditors "would" receive today under a liquidation scenario versus how much they "might" receive in the future under the plan.*

Debt Adjustments

Chapter 13 is a reorganization of an individual's debts. It was originally designed by Congress to provide an alternative to chapter 7 for the wage earner with a regular income who owned property in which he had equity, such as a car or a home. Using chapter 13, the debtor could propose a plan to repay some debts over an extended period of time and renegotiate or eliminate other debts, while retaining the home and car. In a chapter 7, the same debtor would usually lose any equity present in the car or home. Chapter 13 is becoming one of the more commonly used forms of bankruptcy and can be very valuable to the small business owner.

What Debts Are Dischargeable?

All debts that arose prior to the date of filing (called prepetition) are dischargeable in bankruptcy except for ten specific categories of debts prescribed in the Bankruptcy Code.[1]

Debts that are exceptions to discharge (nondischargeable) include those:

- Not listed on the required schedules
- For certain categories of taxes
- Incurred through fraud or false pretenses

---

*Although the bankruptcy courts are supposed to be immune from political and local interests, this is not entirely true. The courts have been known to be loath in election years to order the liquidation of a company if hundreds of employees would be laid off. If your company has local or national business, economic, or political influence, you may receive better treatment in the bankruptcy courts.

- For embezzlement or larceny
- For alimony and child support
- For payments due on payroll withholding and Social Security taxes
- For certain educational loans
- For debts relating to (DWI) offenses, for operating a motor vehicle while under the influence

In a liquidation, when all nonexempt property of the estate has been liquidated or disposed of and all claims by creditors settled, the debtor is granted a discharge (a release) for all debts and obligations listed in the filing except nondischargeable debts.

In the simplest form of bankruptcy reorganization (chapter 11), the debtor has 120 days after filing a petition seeking relief to file a plan of reorganization. This plan must be accepted by the creditors and confirmed by the court.* The effect of the confirmation order is the same as the discharge granted a liquidation filer except that the reorganized debtor remains under the direction of the court to monitor the implementation of the plan. Following the final distribution to creditors, the court enters a final decree ending the bankruptcy.

Priorities in Bankruptcy

Not all claims against the debtor are given equal priority by the bankruptcy court to receive payment. Claims are divided into two categories: secured and unsecured. Unsecured claims are further divided into classifications according to the priority in which they will be paid.

Secured claims are those for which the debtor has pledged property as security for the amounts due. The type of property used as security is usually real estate, vehicles, jewelry, office equipment, or saleable inventory, but can include almost any property, including future revenues, accounts receivable, bank

---

*The process of acceptance of a plan of reorganization is complex. See Bankruptcy Code, 11 U.S.C. § 1126 for complete details.

Exhibit 11-1. Priorities in bankruptcy for paying unsecured claims.

Priority	Description
First:	*Administrative expenses* associated with the bankruptcy; costs of preserving the estate; taxes incurred by the estate (after the filing); professional (legal and accounting) and trustee fees.
Second:	*Debts incurred in the ordinary course of business* after filing date but before appointment of trustee.
Third:	*Back wages,* commissions, and sick pay earned in the last ninety days up to a maximum of $2,000 per employee (including withholding taxes, social security, and state and local taxes on same).
Fourth:	*Employer contributions to employee benefit plans* earned in the last 180 days, but not to exceed $2,000 per employee when combined with payments made to employees under third priority claims (including withholding taxes, social security, and state and local taxes on same).
Fifth:	*Special priority to protect creditors who are farmers and fishermen* for their property held in grain storage facilities, grain processing facilities, and fish storage and processing plants.
Sixth:	*Consumer protection* for down payments and deposits made for rental or purchase of property up to a maximum of $900 per claim.
Seventh:	*Taxes,* including federal, state, and local income, employment, excise, and sales taxes for prior three years; property taxes for prior year; and all trust fund taxes.
Eighth:	All other unsecured claims.

accounts, and works of art. If the debtor fails to make payments or defaults on the terms of the indebtedness for which the property is security, then the creditor has the right to repossess the property.

For a debt to be secured a security agreement is required. This agreement is a legal document with a specific description of the property and the value of the debt for which the property is being used as security. Without a security agreement, the claimant cannot, in bankruptcy, assert an interest in the property that is superior to that of other creditors.

Although not required, most creditors also file a copy of this security agreement with the state or local records authorities (in most states this is usually the Secretary of State or Commissioner of Corporations and the County Clerk). This filing under the uniform commercial code (UCC) is called a UCC-1 filing. If two parties have a secured claim on the same property description, then the claimant with the earliest UCC filing date is superior.

When a debtor files for bankruptcy, a secured creditor can make application to the court for possession of the property used as security. If the value of this property is in excess of the amount due the creditor, then the surplus is required to be returned to the bankrupt estate. More commonly, the value of the property is less than the amount due the creditor, and the creditor is undersecured. The amount of the creditor's claim that is in excess of the property's value will be treated as a nonpriority unsecured claim (the last to be paid).

All other claims are *unsecured* and are divided by the bankruptcy code into eight categories of priorities for being paid.[2] Exhibit 11-1 details each of the priorities described by the code. Funds available to pay unsecured creditors are applied to claims beginning with those in the first priority and must be paid in full before any claims with second priority can be paid, and so forth until all priority claims have been paid. Any claims not falling into any one of the described classes are paid only after all priority claims have been paid.

Voluntary Bankruptcy

Exhibit 11-2 looks at a voluntary business bankruptcy proceeding from three perspectives: (1) the process under which the debtor is operating, (2) the status of the bankruptcy from the court's administrative view, and (3) the status of the debtor.

Exhibit 11-2. Stages of a voluntary business bankruptcy proceeding.

Process	Bankruptcy Status from Court's Administration View		Debtor's Status
Hire Professionals.			Prepetition
Prepare filing.	Case number assigned		Filing of Petition
Operations are restricted	Automatic stay granted.		Postpetition ▲ ↓ ↓
	Liquidations	Reorganizations	
★★ ✍ ★★	Estate liquidated	Plan proposed	PENDENCY OF BANKRUPTCY PROCEEDING
while under the control of the bankruptcy court or appointed trustee.	Distribution to creditors	Plan accepted and confirmed	
	Discharge granted		Discharged.
	Unrestricted operations	Distributions to creditors	
	★★ ✍ ★★	Final decree entered	▼
		Unrestricted operations	

1. *The process under which the debtor is operating.* Prior to a voluntary bankruptcy, the debtor usually hires professionals (turnaround consultants, attorneys, and accountants) and evaluates the option of bankruptcy. When the decision has been made, the petition and supporting schedules are prepared and filed with the bankruptcy court.

The debtor's estate remains under the control of the bankruptcy court until a discharge is granted in a liquidation or a final decree is entered in a reorganization.

2. *The status of the bankruptcy from the court's administrative view.* The first notice that the bankruptcy court has of a debtor voluntarily requesting relief is the receipt of a petition. The

clerk's response, if all (or most of) the required forms are present, is to assign the petition a bankruptcy case number. The debtor is then granted, by statute, an automatic stay, without the need to apply.

In a liquidation, the court appoints a trustee who settles claims of creditors, collects and liquidates the property of the estate, and makes distributions to the creditors. Following a final distribution of payments to the creditors, the court grants a discharge.

In a reorganization, one or more committees of creditors are formed, meetings are held, a trustee is appointed, and a plan of reorganization is proposed. Plans are usually debated, modified and eventually accepted by the creditors and confirmed by an order of the court. Confirmation of the plan of reorganization is the equivalent of a discharge. The court continues to administer the bankrupt estate until a final distribution is made to the creditors and a final decree has been entered.

3. *The status of the debtor.* Prior to a debtor's filing a petition for relief and receiving a bankruptcy case number, the debtor is termed prepetition. After receipt of the case number, the debtor is postpetition. The debtor remains in the pendency of a bankruptcy proceeding until he receives a discharge in a liquidation or a final decree has been entered in a reorganization.

Involuntary Bankruptcy

An involuntary bankruptcy is where three or more entities with claims against the same debtor, of which $5,000 in the aggregate is undisputed, jointly file a petition with the bankruptcy court requesting relief under chapter 7 (liquidation) or chapter 11 (reorganization). The petitioners must state the amount and nature of their claims and certify their belief that the debtor is generally not paying his obligations as they become due. However, a debtor need not be insolvent to be placed into bankruptcy.

Those petitioning for involuntary relief for a debtor that is a troubled company under chapter 7 (liquidation) can be pursuing several strategies, including:

- They may want to receive better value for their claims if the company were liquidated today than continue to allow the business to operate and see a further diminution of the value of the company and possibly their collateral.
- They may want the troubled company to operate under a chapter 11 plan of reorganization but lack the expertise necessary to propose their own plan. A chapter 7 liquidation filing is an inexpensive method of forcing the capable but financially troubled debtor to convert the filing to a chapter 11 and propose a plan of reorganization that is acceptable to the creditors.
- They may want to purchase a valuable asset of the troubled company at a distress sale price.
- They may want to compel the debtor under the penalties of federal bankruptcy laws to reveal the disposition of all of the property of the bankrupt estate.

A petition for involuntary relief for a debtor that is a troubled company under chapter 11 (reorganization) can also be made to pursue several strategies, including:

- To impose a plan of reorganization on a troubled company, usually with new directors and new management talent
- To force the debtor to defend himself by developing and proposing his own plan of reorganization
- To purchase a valuable asset of the troubled company at a distress sale price
- To compel the debtor under the penalties of federal bankruptcy laws to reveal the disposition of all of the property of the bankrupt estate

The troubled company's creditors can use a bankruptcy filing to recover property, gain control of a desired market, and/or punish the principals.

When a company has concealed, transferred, or sold property of the bankrupt estate, an involuntary bankruptcy filing can be a powerful weapon in the hands of a knowledgeable creditor. These are usually creditors who have in-depth knowledge of the

putes. A defensive strategy that incorporates this condition is to make the payments necessary to all creditors "current" and inform creditors in writing where a bona fide dispute exists that the company's failure to make a timely payment is a result of the dispute.

There is no requirement to settle any outstanding disputes to avail your company of the defense of nonpayment for reasons of a disputed claim.** The dispute must, however, not be contrived or an invention to avoid a genuine debt. However, consider that a dispute over $100 of goods back ordered or delivered late as part of a $1,000 invoiced shipment may still give the company the right to withhold or contest payment due on the entire invoice.

The Bankruptcy Code specifies that for a claim to be disputed, the dispute must be bona fide. There is a wealth of prior bankruptcy case law defining what is considered a *bona fide* dispute.[3] Consult your attorney on the court's potential view of your disputed claims.

Examine the company's list of undisputed accounts payable (and any additional claimants) to find the cost of becoming current on all undisputed debts. Consult your attorney as often as required, but try (at least at this stage) to negotiate the payment schedules yourself. Your company will probably have better luck with negotiations being handled from one businessperson to another than by involving counsel. (Remember that in negotiations with creditors you have at least three arrows in your quiver and if you don't try to use all of them, you are wasting valuable resources. You should first try to achieve your negotiation goals by having your bookkeeper negotiate with your creditor's bookkeeper. Then, try to negotiate yourself. Finally, ask your lawyer to use her skills.)

There is no value to be gained in working out arrangements with half the company's creditors if there are insufficient funds to make the other half current. Start with a budget and negotiate

** In the case In *Matter of Busick,* 831 F.2d 745, 17 C.B.C.2d 788 (7th Cir. 1987), the 7th Circuit held that "In assessing whether there is a bona fide dispute, the court need only determine whether there is an objective basis for either a factual or legal dispute as to the validity of the debt. The court need not determine the possible outcome of the dispute."

with the most intransigent creditors first. If the sum of the negotiations exceeds the budget, then the company cannot afford the cost of using this defense to have the involuntary petition dismissed.

When the company has reached agreements with all creditors, make the necessary payments and obtain a written statement from each. The statement should say that the creditor has done business with the company for x years and that the company is generally current with payments on amounts owed. This is not as difficult as you might foresee. If $1 million was formerly due to a creditor and he agrees to a new repayment schedule where you will pay $100,000 a month starting next month, your relationship can now be described as "generally current."

> *Warning:* Making payments to creditors after the receipt of a summons and involuntary petition is a double-edged sword. If you don't make any payments, then you will not be current on your debts. However, if you don't have sufficient funds in the kitty, you will never survive bankruptcy intact.

Following the receipt of the summons your company should make *no* payments to *any* creditor except those absolutely necessary to remain in business until the date of the hearing scheduled on the petition. *Consult closely with your attorney on this matter.*

If the company is unable to prevail in dismissing the petition, then even contractual payment obligations may no longer be a prudent use of the company's limited funds. Furthermore, any payments made ninety days before an order for relief is entered are considered *preferences* and the court may later direct the recipient to return the payments to the bankrupt estate. (Preferences will be discussed in detail later in the chapter.)

Strategy 3: Convert the Bankruptcy to Another Chapter Of Your Liking

The debtor has the onetime statutory right to convert a case involuntarily filed under one chapter to a case under another chapter at *any time*. This right, however, is only available *once* for each debtor. Congress was so concerned about a debtor's right to choose his own type of relief that a sentence was added to the Code in the Bankruptcy Reform Act of 1978 saying that if the debtor waives the right to convert, the waiver is unenforceable.[4]

Although the Bankruptcy Code guarantees the debtor the right to convert to another chapter, it also makes clear that the debtor must be eligible to be a debtor under the desired chapter.[5]

If the case originated under another chapter and was already converted, then the debtor no longer has the right to convert. The debtor may still make a motion to convert, but the court will decide the motion in the best interests of the creditors and not based on the rights of the debtor.

Creditors, other parties in interest, and the bankruptcy court all have the right to object to a debtor's motion to convert a bankruptcy to another chapter, but their objections can be only on the narrow question of whether the debtor is eligible to be a debtor under the desired chapter. This issue of eligibility can result in heated courtroom battles involving debtors motioning for conversion and creditors and other parties in interest objecting.

Parties in interest (other than the debtor) can make a motion to convert the filing to another chapter and the court will entertain the motion, but the decision will be based on what is best for all creditors, not just the party making the motion. (In legal terminology the party making the motion is called the moving party.) Unless the moving party is the debtor, the court will require the posting of a bond by the moving party before considering the motion.

The potential for a courtroom battle with creditors contesting a debtor's motion to convert is why a debtor should retain the services of an experienced bankruptcy attorney. Most bankruptcy attorneys can handle a simple business or personal bankruptcy filing, but not all bankruptcy attorneys are experienced at moving in court to have an involuntary filing dismissed or motioning the court to have an involuntary filing converted to another chapter under adverse scrutiny.

There are two types of conversion.

1. *Convert a chapter 7 to a chapter 11 or 13.* Most involuntary filings are requests for relief by creditors to liquidate the company under chapter 7. The best defense for a troubled company after failing to obtain a dismissal of an involuntary chapter 7 filing is to make a motion before the court to convert the bankruptcy to a reorganization (chapter 11) or debt adjustment (chapter 13) under the Bankruptcy Code. By converting the bankruptcy to one of these two chapters, the company could probably retain control of its destiny and avoid a rapid liquidation.

2. *Convert a chapter 11 to a chapter 7 or 13.* Less common are involuntary bankruptcy filings requesting relief as chapter 11 reorganizations. In the unlikely case of a business having been served with an involuntary chapter 11 petition that is also eligible to be a debtor under chapter 13, the business would usually be better off by making a motion to the court to convert to a chapter 13.*

Although the debtor would always have the onetime statutory right to convert from a chapter 11 to a chapter 7 filing, it is difficult to see any advantage to the company except to use it as a threat to coerce creditors to agree to modifications to a proposed plan of reorganization.

Business or Personal Bankruptcy?

For a small business, the distinctions between what obligations are debts of the business and what are personal debts can become very cloudy. For example, you may have purchased your

---

*There were several bills proposed in Congress in 1993 that would change chapter 13 from the present limitations of less than $100,000 of unsecured debt and less than $350,000 of secured debt. These proposals include raising the ceiling to $1 million without any distinction between secured and unsecured debts. The effect of these changes, if approved by Congress and enacted as law, would make conversion to a chapter 13 from an involuntary bankruptcy filed under chapter 7 or 11 a more common occurrence.

vidual who voluntarily files a bankruptcy petition. (Chapter 12, "Adjustment of Debts of a Family Farmer with Regular Annual Income," is also available if the debtor qualifies. The definition of farming activity was broadened by Congress in The Bankruptcy Judges, United States Trustees, and Family Farmer Act of 1986. In deciding what chapter of the Bankruptcy Code to use, individuals should consider three questions:

1. Under which chapters are they eligible to be a debtor?
2. What are the causes of the potential bankruptcy filing?
3. What are they trying to protect by filing for bankruptcy?

Getting Personal Legal Counsel

An important and early step for the individual who is a principal of a troubled company is to retain personal legal counsel. The Bankruptcy Code does not require that an individual be represented by a lawyer to file a petition under chapter 7 or 13, but it is a prudent strategy to consult an attorney even if you decide not to use one for the filing.

Your personal attorney should not necessarily be the same as the bankruptcy counsel for the company. Sometimes, the company's counsel would have a conflict of interest that would prohibit her from representing both the principal of a company and the company. Discuss your potential personal bankruptcy with at least two other qualified attorneys before deciding to use the same personal bankruptcy counsel as your company.

Achieving Your Goals with Bankruptcy?

If the causes of your present dilemma are personal liability for debts such as fraud, larceny, unpaid payroll withholding taxes, or past due sales taxes, none of which are dischargeable debts under the Bankruptcy Code, then a personal bankruptcy filing may not alleviate your problems. Also, if you have guaranteed certain obligations of the company such as leases and credit lines, it may be possible to work an out-of-court settlement with the creditor that will eliminate the present need for a bankruptcy filing.

Did you cosign for joint responsibility on leases or lines of credit? There may be alternatives depending on the flexibility of the creditor. The threat of your filing for bankruptcy may be enough leverage to work out settlements with the creditors.

What are you trying to protect? Do you own a home, an expensive car, a boat, or an airplane? Do you have another business that might be affected? Are you certain that your unsecured creditors can take action against your home? In Florida, for example, an unsecured creditor cannot force the sale of your home.

Because you can file a chapter 7 bankruptcy only once every six years, carefully consider all of your options before making any decision. If you file for relief under chapter 7 today, some unforeseen future circumstance might require you to file for bankruptcy three years from now, and the option would not be available.

We suggest that you carefully list *all* of your present liabilities and *all* of your assets, including all property that you hold an interest in. Discuss these lists with your personal bankruptcy counsel before making any decisions.*

Using Your Leverage as a Debtor

Threatening to file for bankruptcy may be almost as effective in coercing your creditors to accept settlements as actually making a filing. Work with your bankruptcy counsel to plan what would happen to each of your creditors under a bankruptcy scenario and then use the results as a point of negotiation with your creditors.

Remember that after you file for bankruptcy every creditor (and the rest of the world) will know your complete list of assets and liabilities. If you are planning to file anyway, it can't hurt,

---

*When listing the property that constitutes your estate, ask your attorney for a copy of the definitions of "Property of the Estate" found in the Bankruptcy Code, 11 U.S.C. § 541. When listing the claims against your estate, refer to the Bankruptcy Code, 11 U.S.C. § 105(5) for the definition of "claim." When evaluating potential claims, attention should be given to Bankruptcy Rule 3001, "Proof of Claim," which details the proof required in a bankruptcy proceeding for an entity or individual to assert and to prove a claim against your estate.

as a last-ditch attempt, to reveal some or all of the information to a stubborn creditor to convince him to accept a settlement.

Considering Personal Bankruptcy Chapters

Chapter 7

Chapter 7 is a straight liquidation through bankruptcy and has the advantages of low cost, a speedy discharge, and a minimum of required documentation. The major disadvantages of a chapter 7 are the limitation of filing only once every six years and the personal property that an individual is entitled to keep outside of the bankrupt estate, called exempt property. Lists of exempt properties were prescribed in the Bankruptcy Code,* but Congress gave each state the option of either adopting the federal exemptions or opting out of the federal exemptions and legislating it's own exemptions.

The descriptions of what personal property is considered exempt are different in each state. Some states include as exempt property such as fodder for farm animals, firearms, church pews, sewing machines, fuel for stoves, wedding rings, and family burial plots. Other states put an aggregate value limitation upon personal property without regard to the specific descriptions. In New York, only $10,000 of the value of a personal residence is considered exempt property. In Florida and Texas, a person's entire homestead, even if worth millions of dollars, is exempt.

Chapter 11

In some states (namely Florida and Georgia) the courts have permitted individuals in business to file under chapter 11 to reorga-

*Bankruptcy Code, 11 U.S.C. § 522 Exemptions. Unless otherwise limited by state law, section (b) grants the debtor the right to choose between the exemptions prescribed in section (d) or the exemptions he is entitled to under other federal law and the law of the state in which the filing is made. Exemptions included under other federal law include certain government pensions, Social Security, and retirement payments.

nize since the enactment of the Bankruptcy Code in 1978, but the practice has not been uniform in all states.

In 1991 the U.S. Supreme Court, in *Toibb v. Radloff,* affirmed the right of an individual to file for bankruptcy protection under chapter 11, even if the individual was not engaged in a business. Individuals who previously had limited options to reorganize now became eligible for relief as chapter 11 debtors. On the day following the 1991 Supreme Court decision, *The New York Times* reported, "[The] ruling makes chapter 11 an attractive alternative for individuals who have relatively large debts and relatively large income, or at least the expectation of future income with which to finance a repayment plan."[7]

Chapter 11 filings by individuals are still not common because of the high administrative costs and expenses. Most individuals petitioning for relief under chapter 11 have personally guaranteed extensive business obligations such as real estate mortgages, and the filing is a means to protect their remaining property from seizure by creditors trying to enforce these guarantees.

Even an individual chapter 11 is very expensive and the process can be very time-consuming for the debtor. Don't be mistaken that because you guaranteed debts of the company you must file for bankruptcy to protect your remaining assets. If you are married, have few assets other than your personal residence, or live in a community property state, you may not need to file for bankruptcy to protect your residence. (Some states, including Florida, Vermont, Kansas, Iowa, Minnesota, South Dakota, Oklahoma, and Texas, exempt the homestead from the collection efforts of unsecured creditors. In other states where a residence is the joint property of a married couple, creditors may be prevented from forcing the sale of the property if only one spouse is the judgment debtor.)

Chapter 13

Depending on the amount of an individual's debts, a chapter 13 filing may be significantly less cumbersome and less expensive than a chapter 11 while providing similar relief. Chapter 13, or debt adjustment, is essentially a personal reorganization of individual or family debts. Congress intended chapter 13 to provide relief to an individual debtor or an individual debtor and his or her spouse who were not eligible or could not afford to file for a chapter 11, but would lose too much in a straight chapter 7 liquidation.

The most significant advantage that a chapter 13 debt adjustment has over a chapter 11 reorganization is that the debtor is not required to have the approval of creditors for a repayment plan to be confirmed. In a chapter 13 case, the debtor proposes a plan that needs to be approved only by the U.S. trustee. Although the courts (and the unsecured creditors) would like to see plans that include payments to the unsecured creditors, these payments are not required. Chapter 13 debtors have a significant degree of flexibility in structuring their plans to enable them to develop a feasible repayment plan under which creditors are paid over an extended period under court supervision.

However, under the current law, only debtors with unsecured debts of less than $100,000 and secured debts of less than $350,000 are eligible to file under chapter 13. The debtor must also prove he has a regular source of income (wages, commissions, or other earnings that are the result of his *active** participation in an enterprise) to fund payments due under the proposed plan.

A debtor can typically retain his home and cars while discharging his unsecured consumer debts (credit card, etc.). Although it is strongly recommended that a debtor discuss a potential chapter 13 filing with a bankruptcy attorney, the debtor is not required to use an attorney when making the filing.

Chapter 13 Debtor Eligibility Requirements

1. Individual, or individual and spouse
2. Business debt as long as the business is individually owned
3. No corporations, partnerships, or stock and commodity brokers eligible
4. Source of regular income (wages, commissions, or other

---

*Income such as rent or interest payments has usually been treated by the courts as "passive" and not "active" income.

regular income that is the result of an individual's active participation in an enterprise)

5. Unsecured debts less than $100,000
6. Secured debts less than $350,000
7. Debtor has not participated in a filing before the bankruptcy court during the last 180 days that was dismissed for technical reasons

Advantages of a Chapter 13 Bankruptcy

Approval of the creditors is not required in a chapter 13 bankruptcy. Also, third parties who cosigned or guaranteed obligations of the debtor (often family members) are not held responsible by the renegotiation of the debt. Certain debts not dischargeable in a chapter 7 can be discharged in a chapter 13. These debts include some taxes and debts incurred through false financial statements, fraud, or breach of fiduciary duties. Even for those debts that are nondischargeable, the payments terms can be stretched out and interest and tax penalties can be avoided. Most late charges, interest, and penalties incurred by default can be eliminated.

Where the debtor has concealed assets, fraudulently conveyed property, or is unable to account for assets, the court is much less likely to object or concern itself, although the court does not approve of this conduct.[8]

Debtors who cannot file a chapter 7 because they already filed within the previous six years still have the option of filing a chapter 13.

Filing Sequential Bankruptcies

Contrary to popular belief, not all voluntary forms of bankruptcy prohibit a debtor from filing again before six years has elapsed. However, the law was not uniformly administered by all districts until a 1991 U.S. Supreme Court case, *Johnson v. Home State Bank*. Of significant benefit to small business owners is that *Johnson* affirmed the Court's view that a debtor who has received a discharge in a chapter 7 proceeding has the right to make a sub-

Exhibit 11-5. Waiting periods for serial voluntary bankruptcy filings.

First Filing Chapter	Second Filing Chapter		
	7	11	13
7	6 years	6 years	None
11	6 years	None	None
13	6 years	None	None
Dismissal	180 days	180 days	180 days

sequent chapter 13 filing to protect remaining property from creditors holding nondischarged claims. (These filings are known as chapter 20s: chapter 7 + chapter 13.)*

Exhibit 11-5 shows the necessary waiting periods for serial bankruptcy filings.

Some debtors operate under chapter 11 plans of reorganization, receive a final decree, and later seek new protection under a new plan of reorganization. One example of this type of debtor behavior was the former Braniff Airlines. (See Exhibit 11-6.)

In its first life, the original debtor company, Braniff Airways, Inc., filed a petition requesting relief under chapter 11 in late 1983. The airline was reorganized as Braniff, Inc. (second life), and continued to fly for six years until the fall of 1989, when it filed again for bankruptcy protection under chapter 11. After ceasing operations in late 1989, the airline was reorganized as Braniff International Airlines (third life) and started flying again in 1991, though promptly filing for the protection of chapter 11.

This last reincarnation of a proud company that had once been the thirteenth largest U.S. airline lasted until July 1992,

---

*With no lack of prohibition for serial chapter 13 filings, some individuals have made repeated filings in a relatively short period of time. The lawyers and judges handling these cases have developed their own nomenclature for serial filers. According to one newspaper report, bankruptcy professionals call three successive chapter 13s a chapter 39; add a fourth and it's called a chapter 52. See Bernice Stengle, "Going to Court Again and Again . . ." *St. Petersburg Times*, January 26, 1992, p. 1.

Exhibit 11-6. The three lives of Braniff Airlines.

FIRST LIFE
Braniff Airways,
Inc., 13th largest
U.S. airline, files
chapter 11 in 1983.   SECOND LIFE
Reorganized   Braniff, Inc.
operations continue as: → Operates 1984–1989.   THIRD LIFE
                            Files chapter 11 and   Braniff
                            ceases operations.   International
                            Reorganized as: → Airlines.
                                                     Operates 1991–1992.
                                                     Files chapter 11 and
                                                     ceases operations.
                                                     Is converted to
                                                     chapter 7 and
                                                     liquidated.

---

when it ceased operations. Braniff International Airlines' last bankruptcy was converted to a chapter 7 and is currently in the final stages of liquidation.

The Importance of Deadlines

The rules of the bankruptcy court are very specific about the deadlines for receiving each of the scheduled submissions of documents. Depending on the type of relief sought, the court requires the filings of specific forms and documents describing the assets and liabilities of the debtor and his estate. In a reorganization, the debtor must also show his future ability to pay his obligations.

> *Warning:* Failure by a debtor to meet any of the scheduled deadlines for submission of documents can be considered bad faith and is grounds for the court to dismiss the bankruptcy filing.

Following the dismissal of a bankruptcy petition, the debtor's estate loses the protection of the automatic stay and the debtor remains ineligible to file for *any* form of bankruptcy protection until 180 days have elapsed.

Small Business Bankruptcies and Trust Fund Taxes

Common liabilities in small and medium-size business failures are unpaid taxes including: payroll withholding taxes (city, state, and federal), federal unemployment insurance (FUTA), Social Security and Medicare taxes (FICA), and state sales taxes. These types of taxes that begin their life as corporate responsibilities (i.e., liabilities of the company) can quickly become the personal liabilities of "responsible persons" in the business should the company fall behind on its payments.

It is a frequent occurrence. A company is struggling to survive and all cash flow is being used to purchase goods for sale and to pay salaries. The company falls further and further behind on rent, payroll taxes, and insurance. The company eventually fails and closes its doors. The story might end there except that state and federal laws hold "responsible" persons liable for certain types of past due taxes.

Taxes that a company collects from employees and customers and then holds in trust for the government are called trust fund taxes. When a company fails to make regular payments for trust fund taxes, any (or all) of the responsible persons of the company (bookkeepers, managers, officers, and principals) can be held jointly and severally liable for the full amount of the past due taxes. (If the taxes are due to the Internal Revenue Service, there is also the possibility of the IRS accessing a 100 percent penalty assessment plus interest on any unpaid amounts.)[9]

Although a business can file a petition requesting relief under chapter 7 or 11 of the Code, the liabilities for the company's trust fund taxes are not dischargeable in a bankruptcy.

Trust fund taxes are also entitled to special treatment as priority creditors in bankruptcy and are paid before most other classes of creditors.

Following a company's discharge from bankruptcy, the responsible persons in a company can be held personally liable for any amounts remaining due and owing on these trust fund taxes. In a business bankruptcy, the IRS is not even required to wait until a discharge has been granted or a final decree entered to initiate collection procedures against responsible persons for trust fund tax obligations.

"Chapter 20": A New Option for Small Businesses

So-called chapter 20 (a chapter 7 liquidation followed by a chapter 13 debt adjustment) can be a valuable recourse to the principals of small or medium-size businesses where the principals have personal obligations that are nondischargeable in a chapter 7 bankruptcy.

Persons responsible for obligations of the company that they personally guaranteed can file a petition under chapter 7 to discharge their personal liabilities. However, the obligation to pay the trust fund taxes and other obligations are nondischargeable and survive a chapter 7 bankruptcy. After receiving a discharge, the individual's property can still be levied upon or seized to satisfy these obligations.

One refuge available to the individual with personal liability for trust fund taxes is to file a chapter 13 petition to obtain the protection of the automatic stay. The automatic stay would prevent even the IRS from enforcing collection procedures during the two-to-five-year pendency of the chapter 13 proceeding.

As a chapter 13 debtor, the individual could propose an extended repayment plan for some, all, or none of the trust fund taxes. The degree to which these trust fund obligations can be reduced or eliminated in a chapter 13 bankruptcy depends on the repayment plan approved by the bankruptcy court.

Although there are local (district) rules on how the court should treat trust fund tax obligations, the Code gives significant powers of discretion to each bankruptcy judge to decide based on the facts present in each case.

Even the Government Needs to File a Claim

The government, like all creditors, is required to file a claim to be scheduled for payment in a bankruptcy—in this situation, for payment of taxes. Often, the IRS files claims or modifications to claims late. The courts are lenient with the IRS in accepting tardy submissions, particularly where trust fund taxes are the source of the claim. But repeatedly, the courts have held that the IRS *must* file a claim to be included in the plan.

Where the IRS does file a claim, it is typically "strikingly high" and then "whittled down substantially in negotiations."[10] This practice may be changing. In the recent case of bankrupt retailer R. H. Macy & Company, the debtor negotiated an agreement with the IRS that reduced the estimated $1 billion in back taxes owed by the company to $230 million. However, don't expect your business to have the same leverage as Macy's unless you also owe the IRS $1 billion.

If the business owed state sales taxes or other state or local taxes that are trust fund obligations and these obligations were transferred to the shoulders of the responsible persons in the business, then the state and locality also need to file claims in a chapter 13 proceeding.

What if the government—the IRS or other taxing authority—fails to file a claim in a chapter 13 proceeding? When this happens, the government loses its right to collect.

However, the catch is that if the IRS fails to file a claim but prior to the bankruptcy filed a Notice of Federal Tax Lien, then it can collect on those taxes listed on the lien, but not until after the provisions of the automatic stay are lifted (i.e., when the chapter 13 case is finished). Since a chapter 13 debt repayment schedule typically extends over a period of two to five years, the debtor has ample time to negotiate a settlement with the IRS.

Since the only claims the IRS can have against a discharged chapter 13 debtor are those based on the prepetition federal tax lien, the IRS can collect only from property that the debtor owned prior to the filing (prepetition). This means that any accumulation of wealth by the individual subsequent to the filing (postpetition) is protected from the IRS's collection efforts. This prepetition limitation can provide the debtor with additional leverage when negotiating with the IRS. *Always use your leverage when negotiating with creditors. After filing a chapter 13 petition you have additional leverage when negotiating with the IRS.*

If the property owned by the debtor before she filed the bankruptcy petition is considered nonexempt* from levy by the IRS and is worth less than the amount of the federal tax lien, then the maximum amount the IRS could collect would be the value of the property. Using this amount as a starting point, the debtor has leverage and several years to work out a settlement with the IRS.

Most nonfederal taxing authorities do not have the resources to respond to notices in bankruptcy proceedings and usually don't file claims unless the amount due is very large. If the bankruptcy filing was made outside the state in which the obligations were incurred, then there is only a remote chance the state or local governmental taxing authority will file a claim.

Taxes and Chapter 13 Confirmation

The IRS rarely objects to confirmation of a chapter 13 plan. It is unknown if this is done as a matter of IRS policy or for lack of resources.

When ruling on a chapter 13 debtor's repayment plan, the judge can confirm the plan as is, confirm it with modifications, or return it to the debtor for additional modifications. If a debtor declares in the proposed plan that repayment of the full amount of the tax debt would place an undue hardship on the debtor (and his or her family), then the court has it within its authority to eliminate all or part of the claim. Although courts have been reluctant to eliminate 100 percent of a trust fund tax debt, they may eliminate the part that would have remained unpaid after the three-to-five-year term of the repayment plan.

The courts have been instructed that the congressional in-

---

*"Exempt property" as used in this context refers to property that the IRS treats as exempt from levy in collection proceedings, not the definition of property treated as exempt under state or federal law relating to bankruptcy. See IRS Publication No. 586A titled "The Collection Process (Income Tax Accounts)."

tent present in the Bankruptcy Code was to provide special treatment for trust fund taxes. The result is that the courts do not generally discharge a debtor's responsibility for these taxes, but in the alternative may discharge penalties, accumulated interest, or other personal income taxes to alleviate the hardship imposed by the aggregate amount of the tax claims.

State and local governmental taxing authorities' objections to confirmations of chapter 13 plans are an even rarer occurrence than objections by the IRS. If the bankruptcy is filed outside the state in which the obligations were incurred, there is almost no chance that the local governmental authorities will object to a plan's confirmation.

> *Suggestion:* An individual may be eligible to be a resident, or may have the time to acquire residence, in another state. Debtors should carefully evaluate *all* of their debts and obligations and consider the merits of making a filing in the state most advantageous to their personal situation.

Consolidation in Bankruptcy

In cases where either several related businesses or a principal and a business are one and the same and all need to seek bankruptcy protection, each business and individual must file a separate petition. However, your attorney can request that the cases be "consolidated" and administered by the court as if they were one case. The major advantage of consolidation is that it reduces the costs of administrative and professional fees (accountants, lawyers, and consultants) while in bankruptcy. Be aware that creditors or other parties in interest can also request that the court consolidate cases. Consolidation may not always be to the advantage of the individual.

If there are disputes among the principals or the related businesses, or not all related businesses share the same group of shareholders, there may be disadvantages to consolidation. Ask your attorney to review the particulars and advise you of the benefits and problems of consolidation.

Warning: Don't forget that a bankruptcy attorney can charge two debtors more for representing two separate cases than one consolidated case and therefore might have a self-interest in keeping the cases separate. Check with more than one attorney if you are uncertain about consolidation.

The Importance of Affiliates, Insiders, Preferences And Fraudulent Transfers

Affiliates

Affiliates are businesses that are in some way related to the debtor or the principal owner, shareholder, or executives of the debtor. The businesses can have different names and addresses, be separate corporations, have different officers, and be in different sectors (manufacturing, farming, retail sales, etc.) and still be affiliates. They can be related by common ownership or control or by sharing property in common. The definition encompasses a broad range of persons and entities.

Affiliates are subject to increased scrutiny during bankruptcy proceedings. During bankruptcy, transfers of property, payments, and revenues can be disguised by unscrupulous debtors using an affiliated entity. To protect creditors, the Code permits a trustee to examine transactions involving affiliates for a year before the date of filing.

As a debtor, don't be too clever and attribute all of your debts to one company and your assets to another entity. If after the original filing the court decides that another business is affiliated and should have been included in the original filing, *all* of the assets of the affiliate can be incorporated into the estate of the debtor.

Failure to make a complete and truthful bankruptcy filing might also result in federal penalties for perjury or fraud. The court also has the authority to dismiss any case where the filing has been made in bad faith.

Insiders

Insiders are a class of persons who by their relationship to the debtor are suspect in that they might receive special treatment from the debtor. As creditors they are likely to be the natural recipient of preferences (i.e., if you owed two creditors and one was your brother, he would be likely to have first priority for being paid). Although insiders naturally include family members of the debtor and principals of the debtor company, they also include principals of affiliates and those who would be considered insiders of the affiliate.

The class of insiders also includes parties who are not directly related but are in control of the debtor. Financial institutions such as banks that exercise too much direct control of a debtor have sometimes been held by the court to be insiders.

To protect the interests of all creditors, the Code sets the period for scrutinizing transactions where preferences might have taken place to ninety days for the general creditor, but it increases the period of scrutiny to one year for transactions involving insiders.

What can insiders do to prepare themselves? The Code paints the definition of an insider with a very broad brush, and the definition of an affiliate requires the interpretation of a skilled professional. It is strongly recommended that you consult an experienced attorney for an interpretation of your company's affiliates and insiders.

Transactions involving insiders will be reviewed by the trustee and the creditors very early in a bankruptcy proceeding. Make certain if there any potential problems that your counsel is aware of the circumstances before your creditors find out.

Preferences

A preference occurs when a creditor, in the period immediately prior to a bankruptcy filing, receives property (or monies) of the debtor in excess of what he would be entitled to receive in the distribution to creditors under the Bankruptcy Code. In a business bankruptcy, a preference is created when, prior to a bankruptcy filing, the debtor pays certain creditors in preference to others. A preference is also created when property of the company, such as a car, is given to or sold for less than fair market value to an officer or other insider of the company. Congressional intent in the design of this section of the Code was "to discourage unusual action by either the debtor or his creditors during the debtor's slide into bankruptcy."[11]

The "look-back" period in evaluating whether a transfer is a preference is only ninety days prior to the date of filing. However, in the case of an insider or affiliate, the look-back period is increased to one year.

> *Warning:* Preferences are not illegal acts per se, but they can be undone by the trustee in bankruptcy. And if the preference is large enough or the intent was blatantly obvious, then the debtor might be charged with fraud. Therefore, careful planning should be made before making any payments that might be treated as preferences in bankruptcy.

If a transfer is considered a preference under the Code, the trustee can "avoid" the transfer. In plain English this means that the trustee can force the recipient of the preference to return the property to the bankrupt estate. Not all preferences can be avoided by the trustee, and the Code lists at least seven types of exceptions. If a preference meets the criteria set forth for any one of the exceptions, then the transfer of property, although still considered a preference, is not avoidable by the trustee.

The most commonly used exception to a trustee avoiding a preference are that the transfer was effected in the "ordinary course of business" or that the debtor received payment (called new value) for the property.

Five Conditions of a Preference

The Code sets five criteria that must all be met for the transfer of property to be considered a preference. The transfer must be:

1. Made within ninety days before the date of the bankruptcy filing or within one year prior of the filing if the creditor was an insider.

2. To or for the benefit of a creditor, even if paid to another party. (Even if the creditor was not the direct recipient of the preference but the debtor paid someone the creditor owed, or paid the creditor's brother-in-law, it is still a preference.)

3. For, or on account of, a debt that arose prior to the transaction. (The debt must be "antecedent"—i.e., owed by the debtor before the transfer was made. If made for current business, payments are not preferences, even if made within the ninety-day or one-year period.)

4. Made while the debtor was insolvent. (If the debtor was not insolvent then, then paying one creditor in preference to another is not prohibited. This is because had the company been liquidated at that instant, there would have been sufficient assets to pay all of the debtor's obligations.)

5. Such that a creditor would receive more than he would receive in a straight bankruptcy liquidation (chapter 7), if the transfer had not been made, and if the debtor filed for bankruptcy later. (If the effect of the preference was that a creditor received payment for 50 percent of the amount due him and in a bankruptcy he would have received the same percentage, then the transfer is not a preference. But where the transfer, for example, depleted inventory to a point where the business became worthless, then the transfer could be considered a preference because the creditor wouldn't have received as much if he had waited in line with the other creditors.)

Exceptions to Avoidance of Preferences

As previously stated, not all preferences can be avoided (undone) by the trustee. The Code prescribes seven exceptions to the preference statute. If a transfer of property to a creditor can qualify under any one of the exceptions, then the transfer is protected from avoidance by the trustee to the extent provided by the exception.

Study your local bankruptcy court's decisions on preferences and exceptions very carefully. If the company has made any extraordinary payments to insiders (during the past year) or to other creditors (during the last ninety days), there may be actions the company can take prepetition to correct the mistake or to mitigate the postpetition ramifications of the payments.

Problems with Preferences

The problems with preferences for a small or medium-size business usually occur under the following circumstances: (1) when property is transferred to or sold to insiders or affiliates; (2) in the ninety-day period prior to a bankruptcy filing when a creditor receives a largess; or (3) when payments are made by the debtor outside the ordinary course of business.

1. *When property is transferred to or sold to insiders or affiliates.* An example of this is the transfer or sale to the insider of a company-owned vehicle driven by the insider. Although the transfer or sale is not prohibited, it must be done for consideration equal to the fair market value of the vehicle. The problem occurs because the transfer is commonly done not in exchange for contemporaneous payment but for monies owed to the insider— that is, an antecedent debt. If the business is insolvent at the time of the transfer, then the insider cannot be awarded special treatment and must stand in line with all of the other unsecured creditors to receive payment. If the insider received special treatment as a creditor, then he was in receipt of a preference that is probably avoidable by the court.

The way to repair these types of preferences is to have the insider return title of the vehicle to the company prior to the bankruptcy filing, or to have the insider pay the company for the fair market value of the vehicle. The payment can be cash, check, or even a promissory note, but it cannot be a used to offset an old debt that preceded the present transaction (antecedent debt).

In the ninety-day period prior to filing for bankruptcy, the debtor must be very careful to avoid making any payments that could be construed as preferences.

2. *When a creditor receives a largess.* An essential vendor who senses that the company is sliding into bankruptcy and requires that all prior debts be paid before any new shipments are made is asking for a preference. A vendor who is a friend of an insider and is paid all past due amounts prior to filing is receiving a preference.

Paying antecedent debts when the company is insolvent or not paying other creditors in the same fashion is usually a preference. The way to avoid these types of preference payments is to make the payments as exceptions to avoidance under the Code.

In the case of the essential vendor, you can pay her on a COD basis for all new shipments, thereby limiting the vendor's future in continuing to do business with your company. COD payments are contemporaneous and are in exchange for new value received and are therefore exceptions to avoidance under the Code.

In the case of a vendor who is a friend, the insolvent company cannot pay antecedent debts without the payments being preferences. However, the insolvent company can make payments on deposit for future purchases. Deposits are payments for future performance and are in exchange for value to be received and are therefore exceptions under the Code.

3. *When payments are made by the debtor outside the ordinary course of business.* These types of preferences can occur in a variety of situations. The payment in a lump sum of annual bonuses, severance pay, or retirement benefits to employees in the ninety days prior to a bankruptcy filing are clearly preferences. Payments in round amounts (e.g., $5,000, $10,000, or $25,000) to vendors where the invoices received from the vendors are rarely in such neat numbers could be construed as preferences.

The way to avoid these types of situations is to have all payments made in the ordinary course of business. If you make any lump-sum payments to employees, one would hope that they are astute enough to spend the monies or, at the least, not leave them in their checking account where they could be found by a bankruptcy trustee.

If you need to pay a vendor $5,000 to continue doing business, then pay several individual invoices with separate checks that in the aggregate are close to $5,000.

Fraudulent Transfers

A fraudulent transfer is a transfer of property of the bankrupt estate that is an attempt by the debtor or other party to defraud the estate's creditors. Fraudulent transfers include those made for less than equivalent value, those made where it was obvious that the debtor was incurring debts beyond his ability to repay, and those made with actual intent to hinder, delay, or defraud a past or future creditor.

The Code grants the trustee the authority to avoid fraudulent transfers that occurred within one year of the date of filing. The trustee may sue to recover property of the estate, and pursuant to other federal statutes the bankruptcy court is granted the right to hold hearings to determine, avoid, or recover any property that may have been fraudulently conveyed.

Where a fraudulent transfer of property appears to have been concealed, the law also grants the court the right to investigate and look back up to four years to determine whether a fraud against the creditors was committed.

> *Warning:* Study your local bankruptcy court's decisions on fraudulent transfers. If the company has made any transfers that might be considered suspect by an outsider, discuss the circumstances with your attorney. There may be actions the company can take today to mitigate the postpetition effects of the suspect transfer.

When Is Bankruptcy Not a Viable Choice?

Bankruptcy is an excellent vehicle to give a fresh start to an individual or a business debtor, as was intended by Congress. However, the public exposure and legal scrutiny that result from a bankruptcy filing are often more than a closely held business can withstand.

During the pendency of a bankruptcy proceeding, the

debtor's life is on display for the world to see. Some observers have said that a debtor's postpetition existence is like life in a fishbowl. The behavior of a closely held company that is usually kept behind closed doors is exposed in a bankruptcy proceeding for the courts and creditors to scrutinize and the world to see.

A voluntary bankruptcy filing may not be a wise choice if the company has potential problems with fraudulent conveyances, preferential payments, false or misleading statements made on loan documents (possible commercial loan fraud), significant personal or corporate tax liabilities, or trust fund tax liabilities.

A bankruptcy under any of the above-mentioned problems could result in additional civil proceedings against the principals or other responsible persons, criminal proceedings against the principals, and the loss of all potentially recoverable value left in the company to the principals.

> *Warning:* Do not mislead your bankruptcy counsel by not telling her about questionable activities of the company or its principals.
>
> If you have creditors with significant claims, they will uncover the dirt on the company and its principals in their efforts to recover on their claims.
>
> Your friends may not know what you did behind closed doors, but your creditors will find out. And once they present their case to the court, the entire world will have full knowledge.

A good bankruptcy attorney should be able to mitigate some situations restricting you from filing or confirm the risks of a filing and advise you in seeking alternative solutions to your company's problems.

Where to File for Bankruptcy

The state in which a debtor is eligible to file for bankruptcy is governed by the federal law relating to jurisdiction and venue. These laws specify that a debtor may file in the district in which the debtor has a domicile, residence, or principal place of business or where his primary assets are located.

The law further requires that the debtor or property must have resided in the district of choice for the last 180 days, or if the period is less than 180 days, then at least longer than the portion of that 180-day period that the debtor or property resided in another district. This means that an individual can establish residency in another state for purposes of a bankruptcy filing in as little as ninety-one days.

The bankruptcy court system is divided into fifty-one jurisdictions (fifty states and the District of Columbia), twelve circuits, and 286 districts. For some debtors, the laws on venue and jurisdiction grant them eligibility to file in more than one state and district. Although the Code is uniform throughout the districts, the interpretation and practice can vary greatly. Some districts are known to be more "pro-debtor" and some have histories of rulings that are more "pro-creditor." A debtor should carefully examine his options and file in the district and state that provide the best treatment for his personal or business situation.

Take the example of Harry the pharmacist who owns and operates Harry's Pharmacy on the south shore of Long Island, New York. For the last ten years, Harry has been living in Florida, where he owns a $400,000 home, for six months of each year. The neighborhood where Harry's Pharmacy is located has changed and the business has become deeply troubled. Since Harry personally guaranteed all of the business debt, both he and the business need to seek the protection of the bankruptcy court.

Harry is eligible to file for bankruptcy in Florida, where he has a residence and a domicile, or in New York, where he has a business property. Harry should consult a knowledgeable bankruptcy attorney, but it is clear that if Harry filed his petition in New York he would lose the advantage of the generous personal and household exemptions available to the debtor in Florida.

The laws in Florida permit the debtor to retain more property than in many other jurisdictions, and the state has even been called a debtor's haven by *The Wall Street Journal*.[12] It takes only ninety-one days to establish residency in Florida, and the state laws allow an individual to keep an extensive list of personal property exempt from the bankrupt estate.

Exempt property includes the debtor's primary residence under the homestead exemption. Unlike many other states, the homestead exemption is not limited to a particular value. The debtor in Florida may also retain her full interest in any retirement funds, IRAs, and the cash surrender value of any life insurance. Another advantage in Florida is that creditors cannot attach or garnish a debtor's wages or bank accounts that are a result of her personal earnings.

Famous individuals who moved their residences to Florida and promptly took advantage of the lenient debtor laws to file for bankruptcy include former baseball commissioner Bowie Kuhn, attorney Harvey Myerson, and investment banker Martin Seigel.

When faced in late 1989 with the imminent bankruptcy of Myerson & Kuhn—the law firm that bore their names—Harvey Myerson and Bowie Kuhn moved to Florida and declared personal bankruptcy. As partners, Kuhn and Myerson were potentially liable for at least $3.1 million in bank loans in addition to other debts of the firm. Both debtors' choice of Florida residency in their bankruptcy filings were unsuccessfully challenged by Myerson & Kuhn's creditors. (Although the creditors' challenge to his Florida residency was unsuccessful, Myerson was later convicted on felony fraud charges related to the bankruptcy of the firm.)

Kuhn sold his $1.2 million home in Ridgewood, New Jersey (where the homestead exemption is only $10,000), and moved to Florida, where he purchased a $1 million home near Jacksonville before filing for bankruptcy as a Florida resident. At the time of his move, creditors of Myerson & Kuhn also claimed that he moved a $2 million investment account to Florida to place it beyond their reach.

Kuhn's move to Florida was so rapid and achieved such notoriety that some legal practitioners have started to call the travel plans of large debtors who flee to Florida "pulling a Bowie Kuhn." A judge in a New York case recently issued an injunction freezing the assets of partners of a failed law firm, saying, "I don't want another Bowie Kuhn moving to Florida."[13]

Myerson also moved to Florida and took advantage of the Florida homestead exemption to purchase a $1.75 million home in the Florida Keys before filing for bankruptcy.

As for Martin Seigel, he was arrested in 1986 on felony charges of conspiracy to break securities laws and tax evasion, to which he pleaded guilty in 1987. He also moved to Florida at a time when creditors would be held at bay by his change in residence. This involved Seigel's selling his $1 million apartment in New York City and purchasing a multimillion-dollar home (exempt from the claims of creditors under Florida law) near Jacksonville. Seigel was convicted in 1990 on felony charges relating to his insider trading activities (along with associates Ivan Boesky and Dennis Levine).

States That Are Best for Filing

The major differences in filing personal bankruptcy from one state to another are the list of what property is considered exempt personal property and the limit for the value of the personal homestead exemption. *For a business bankruptcy, there is no difference in filing for bankruptcy in one state over another.*

Exhibit 11-7 details the wide range of personal property exemptions available by comparing for five property categories the federal, New York, California, and Florida exemptions. Notice that the homestead exemption in Florida is unlimited in value. The only restriction on value is a size limitation of half an acre if

Exhibit 11-7. Comparison of personal property exemptions.

	New York	Florida	Federal
Homestead	$10,000	Unlimited	$7,500
Vehicle	$ 2,400	None	$1,200
Life insurance (loan value)	$ needed for support	Unlimited	$4,000
IRA	None	Unlimited	None
Retirement income	$ needed for support	Unlimited	$ needed for support

the property is in a city and 160 acres if the property is in a rural area. Contrast the unlimited Florida exemption with the federal homestead exemption of $7,500 or the New York statute, which limits the homestead exemption to $10,000! However, where New York exempts $2,400 of the value of a personal motor vehicle, Florida does not provide any exemption for a motor vehicle.

As the exhibit demonstrates, exemptions vary greatly from state to state, and a debtor may be eligible to file in more than one state. Individuals contemplating bankruptcy would be well advised to research the exemptions in the state(s) in which they are eligible and consult a knowledgeable attorney.

How to Plan Your Residence for Bankruptcy

The bankruptcy court has the authority either to dismiss a petition or transfer it to another venue if it finds that a recent change of residence was made only to thwart the claims of creditors. There are a few cases of debtors with large debts incurred in another state moving to Florida and then filing for bankruptcy only to have the court, upon a motion by creditors, transfer the proceeding to the debtor's former state of residence.

The Wall Street Journal reported that Tennessee banker Jake Butcher and his wife were unsuccessful in trying to avail themselves of the Florida homestead exemption in their 1991 bankruptcy filing. The case was transferred to the Butchers' home state of Tennessee.[14]

Given what you have learned about personal property exemptions in Florida and New York, as a prudent businessperson, why would anyone file for personal bankruptcy in New York if she could hold out another few months, legally establish residency in three months in Florida, and file there? With Florida being such a desirable place to retire, and one of the most lenient states in which to file for bankruptcy, debtors can plan for a future bankruptcy by establishing a residence in Florida.

Though it is rare that the bankruptcy court will act upon an individual's change of residence, it can happen. But if you move a year or more before filing, you can probably avoid the legal charge that the change in residence was done to defraud creditors.

What Bankruptcy Means for a Business

Briefly, in a chapter 7 liquidation, bankruptcy means the cessation of all business except that permitted by the trustee to preserve the property and value of the bankrupt estate.

The business of a company in liquidation can be extensive in the case of an airline that needs mechanics to maintain aircraft, accountants to sort out the finances, and even pilots to move planes around. Alternatively, for a small retailer, the requirements may be limited to safeguarding the remaining inventory and fixtures until a buyer can be found.

Where the creditors are aggressive, or a diversion or concealment of assets is suspected, the principals and executives of the debtor are likely to be examined by the creditors and the trustee. If the insiders acted illegally, they may be ordered by the court to return assets. Although these parties are also subject to criminal prosecution, this rarely occurs.* Following the bankruptcy discharge, these executives are free to pursue their lives.

In a chapter 11 reorganization, the business continues to operate and work on a plan of reorganization. Although the bankruptcy filing and the protection gained from the provisions of the automatic stay protect the company from direct attacks by creditors, the war is far from over.

Keeping control of a company that has filed for reorganization is akin to steering a boat through a hurricane. Fewer than 12 percent of all reorganizations succeed, and most die a horribly messy death. They are either slain by angry creditors or by their own lawyers in their first few court appearances and subsequently auctioned to vultures who wait on the courthouse steps for their prey.

Prepare for the worst possible experience of your life, and

---

*Very few debtors are investigated by the office of the U.S. trustee for fraud in bankruptcy, and even fewer are convicted. In the period 1989–1991 there were almost 200,000 personal and business bankruptcy filings in southern California. During the same period, the office of the U.S. trustee achieved criminal convictions in only twelve cases! See Tom Furlong, "Swamped by Debtors and Abuse: The Southern California Bankruptcy System Is Struggling under a Deluge of Cases, Both Legitimate and Fraudulent." *Los Angeles Times*, January 12, 1992, p. A1.

even then it will be worse than you expected. Ask anyone who has been through the experience about the process of filing for reorganization through bankruptcy. The only way to prevent your company from incurring this fate is to prepare everything you will need to succeed before filing and, if at all possible, avoid it.

Employees

Employees who are discharged by a company in bankruptcy can file for unemployment benefits, but they are not expressly guaranteed any other severance benefits.

• *Severance.* Those fortunate employees who were laid off or retired prior to the date of filing or the cessation of the business may be lucky in having received benefits or at the least in having earned priority status for any amounts due them. Except amounts recently earned by and due to employees and stated in the Code as third and fourth priorities, any payments due employees are unsecured claims. All employees holding these nonpriority claims must wait in line with the other unsecured creditors to be paid.

• *Wages.* In enacting the Bankruptcy Code, Congress recognized the priority of wage payments due employees of a failed business. These payments are unsecured claims but may be entitled to a third-priority status.

In a business bankruptcy, the unsecured claims of employees are a priority only if the employees were entitled to payment for wages, salaries, or commissions, or for vacation, severance, or sick pay, and the payment was earned within ninety days of the filing date or the cessation of the debtor's business, whichever occurred first. The Code also places a maximum aggregate benefit on these types of priority payments of $2,000 per individual.

• *Benefits.* The debtor's contribution to employee benefit plans is also treated as a priority if the contribution arises from services rendered within 180 days of the filing date or the cessation of the debtor's business, whichever occurred first. However, the Code imposes a limit under this priority of $2,000 per employee, less any amounts paid to employees as third-priority claims (wages) and less any other payments made by the estate, on behalf of the employee, to any other employee benefit plan (union or guild, etc.).

• *Other payments due employees.* Any other amounts due an employee for work performed beyond the most recent ninety-day period, in excess of $2,000 or in excess of the amounts permitted under fourth-priority payments for employee benefit plans, are treated as unsecured claims and scheduled for payment along with all other unsecured nonpriority creditors.

Customers and Vendors

The question often asked of bankruptcy lawyers is what to do about contracts that say that the customer or vendor can cancel the agreement in the case of a bankruptcy filing by the debtor. Can these parties cancel a contract because of a bankruptcy filing? The answer is a definitive *no!*

These types of clauses appear commonly in contracts and are called ipso facto clauses (meaning matter-of-fact clauses). But because they are contrary to the Bankruptcy Code, they are unenforceable under U.S. law.

This means that a customer or vendor's contractual clause permitting him to terminate a contract by virtue of a debtor's bankruptcy filing conflicts with the Bankruptcy Code, and the debtor or trustee can request the court to issue an order prohibiting the other party from terminating the contract. In addition, any party who terminates a contract simply because of a bankruptcy filing can be liable to the bankrupt estate for any damages caused to the debtor's business.

One recent and clear case of a bankruptcy court enforcing a contract against the wishes of a vendor was the aviation fuel supplier to bankrupt Eastern Airlines. The vendor initially refused to supply additional fuel as required by contract until Eastern paid the antecedent debts for past (prepetition) fuel deliveries. The trustee was forced to obtain an order of the bankruptcy court that enforced the fuel delivery contract, and the supplier complied.

Bankruptcy grants the debtor protection with an automatic

stay and the prohibition against enforcement of ipso facto clauses. This protection is very valuable and is unique to the federal Bankruptcy Code. Orders of the bankruptcy court are enforceable anywhere in the United States and its territories.

Most states have laws and proceedings that parallel the federal bankruptcy laws governing receiverships and insolvency proceedings, but they do not provide the same protection. Most notably, the jurisdiction of a state court, in most cases, is limited to the boundaries of the state. This means that a court-appointed receiver would have very limited powers trying to administer the affairs of a company that had assets and business in more than one state. State laws also grant only limited protection to the debtor from the onslaught of multiple creditors.

A clause in a contract stating that a party can terminate the contract in the event of "insolvency, a receiver being appointed, or a bankruptcy proceeding" is unenforceable if the debtor files for federal bankruptcy protection. But if the company is operating under a receiver appointed by the state courts, the clause may be enforceable.

Receiverships operating under the authority of state law are most useful where one secured creditor controls most of the assets of the debtor. These proceedings are usually less expensive to administer than a chapter 11 reorganization but provide only limited benefits to the debtor.

The types of businesses that would most commonly be in receiverships sanctioned by the state courts are real estate developments where one financial institution holds the primary mortgage or retail stores where one secured creditor provided all of the inventory financing.

Getting Advice in Bankruptcy

Remember Polonius's advice to his son in *Hamlet* and take your own counsel first. Simply because your business has entered a troubled period is no reason to lose confidence in your leadership or business management abilities. You've probably already made the worst mistakes and you are on an uphill journey. The bankruptcy filing may provide the fresh start on your sojourn to the mountaintop and a successful business recovery. You will probably need legal bankruptcy counsel, but don't let the attorney run wild and try to control your life. Use a bankruptcy attorney for legal counsel and representation and not for any other purpose.

The Need for an Attorney

Although it is strongly advised that you always seek the counsel of a competent attorney, an individual making a personal filing under chapters 7 or 13 is not required to be represented by an attorney. You can go to the bankruptcy court, obtain copies of the petition forms, and file these petitions as an individual yourself.

However, it is recommended that you not make bankruptcy filings yourself unless you are knowledgeable about the legal process and the potential liabilities of representing yourself in court. Even if you choose to represent yourself, seek the counsel of a bankruptcy attorney and have him review your petition before you file it with the court.

Unlike an individual, a business is required to be represented by an attorney, although the courts may make some exceptions for sole proprietorships or companies where the principals are attorneys or trained professionals. If your business needs to file for bankruptcy but cannot afford an attorney, the court has it within its authority—although it is rarely used—to appoint an attorney to represent the debtor pro bono (i.e., at no charge to the debtor).

In some states, such as California and Florida, a paraprofessional is permitted to prepare and to make the filing for the bankrupt. The paraprofessional, however, cannot represent you in court.

The Bankruptcy Attorney's Role

The role of a bankruptcy attorney—her business mission, in other words—is to represent your interests before the bankruptcy court and to provide the company with legal counsel about the issues of creditors and bankruptcy. But the bankruptcy attorney should not tell you what to do. As 19th-century financier J. P. Morgan stated, "Well, I don't know as I want a lawyer to tell me what I cannot do. I hire him to tell me how to do what I want to do."

Bankruptcy attorneys usually have a stronger knowledge of accounting and business than other members of the bar, mostly because of the nature of the role they take in proceedings. They often act as if they were experts in business, but debtors must be wary of taking their business advice.

Most lawyers have no prior business experience other than working as an attorney, and unless they are partners in their law firms, they usually have never even been responsible for a weekly payroll. Bankruptcy attorneys may be experienced in the management of bankruptcy cases, but they are rarely qualified to be business advisers or management consultants.

You wouldn't give much credibility to your dentist's advice on executing a new will, and you should not give credence to your attorney's advice on matters that go beyond the legal scope of the bankruptcy filing.

We have asked many bankruptcy attorneys the following question: "If you were asked by a client to give business advice, would you?" All of the attorneys answered that they never give business advice, saying they were not qualified. Several told us that although they had some business experience, they were lawyers—not businesspersons. The answers were what we expected, but anyone who has experience with bankruptcy lawyers would agree that these professionals cross the line and give business recommendations quite willingly.

Unfortunately, many debtors—even those with decades of business experience—because of their predicament and feelings of helplessness, also misplace confidence in their attorneys' business counsel.

But don't place the blame upon your attorney. Would you blame your dentist for giving you poor advice on estate planning? It's your own fault for listening to the advice.

> The failure of lawyers to limit their counsel to the practice of law is usually the result of the client's willingness to listen.

Meeting with a Bankruptcy Attorney

Unless you are facing an imminent problem with a creditor that will impair your ability to conduct business, take the time to prepare for your first meeting with a bankruptcy attorney. A number of documents should be prepared before meeting with a prospective bankruptcy lawyer.

Documents to Prepare Before Meeting
A Bankruptcy Attorney

1. List of all business liabilities, i.e., debts. (Include all accounts payable and all scheduled debts such as loans, mortgages, leases, credit card payments, and utilities.)
2. List of all business assets. (Include all bank accounts, stocks and investments, real estate, vehicles, major equipment, insurance claims due, accounts receivable, deposits, and refunds due.)

For items 1 and 2 initially, to make a filing, the attorney needs only the name of the asset, debtor, or creditor and the amount or value. Eventually the court will require the full name and address for each entry on the lists.

3. All of the obligations that you or other officers, managers, or employees share or cosigned for on behalf of the business.
4. Details of any outstanding litigation or pending arbitration.
5. Copies of leases, contracts, loan documents, guarantees, and all UCC filings (security interests in property).
6. Copies of tax liens or levies.
7. Lists of any recently bounced checks.
8. All checks written and delivered or mailed to the payee that have not yet cleared the bank. (Include payroll and commission checks.)
9. List of all wages, salaries, and commissions that are past due.
10. List of any overdue taxes, particularly any trust fund

taxes (payroll taxes, withholding, Social Security, unemployment insurance, and workers compensation).

In addition, if you or other principals of the business are contemplating a personal bankruptcy filing, you will need personal lists for the items in 1 through 8 of this list.

> *Warning:* Consult your personal attorney before showing any of your personal exhibits to the company's bankruptcy counsel.

All of these documents will make the meeting significantly more effective and should allow the attorney to give you an analysis of your options and a better estimate of the costs involved.

Choosing an Attorney

Shop around! Choosing a bankruptcy attorney is no different from choosing a doctor for your children. You are placing a large part of your financial and business life in the lawyer's hands.

Discuss your case with at least two bankruptcy attorneys before making any decisions. If the attorney or her law firm represents any of your creditors, she may be prohibited by a possible conflict of interest from representing you.

> *Warning:* To make the process of selecting an attorney efficient, the first step should be to show the attorney the debtor's complete list of creditors and potential claimants and ask her if she has any conflicts of interest *before* discussing the merits and the details of the case.

The fees for filing bankruptcy are the same throughout the United States, but this does not apply to the fees you pay your bankruptcy attorney for legal representation both prior to and during the pendency of the bankruptcy proceeding. All legal fees are negotiable and if you are not satisfied with the estimate, then continue shopping.

Paying Professionals

Although prior to filing, a debtor is free to make any mutually agreed upon financial arrangements with an attorney to provide counsel pursuant to a bankruptcy filing, all payments made to attorneys or nonattorneys who assist in the bankruptcy filing are subject to review by the trustee and the court. This is because Congress was concerned about protecting the rights of creditors on payments to professionals. First, the debtor could defraud creditors by overpayments to attorneys and other professionals. Second, attorneys could defraud creditors by demanding an unreasonable fee from a debtor in a vulnerable position.

The major concern over professional fees comes in bankruptcy reorganizations (chapter 11s). Professionals cannot make an application to the court for their fees to be paid by the estate until 120 days after the date of filing. This means that they will demand to be paid *in advance* enough to cover the first 120 days.

If you need to hire both personal and business counsel, then there are two retainers to be paid to attorneys and possibly two retainers to accountants.

Most bankruptcy attorneys and accountants require at least $10,000 each to make even the smallest chapter 11 filing, and retainers of $50,000 to $100,000 are not uncommon. Carefully consider if the advantages of bankruptcy outweigh these considerable costs and the public exposure.

Preparing for a Possible Bankruptcy Filing

Always consult at least one bankruptcy attorney and consider seeking a second opinion before you decide how, when, and where to file for bankruptcy.

When should you time your bankruptcy filing? The advice is similar to that given to the new restaurateur who asked what three factors would make a restaurant successful. The answer is location, location, and location. When should you file for bankruptcy? When you have planned, planned, and planned.

A poorly timed filing is one done after the company has been padlocked by the IRS, been evicted from its offices by the landlord, or had its bank accounts seized by a judgment creditor. A filing done after any of these actions can still be useful, but doing it the week before would have been better timing.

If you owe most of your bills at the beginning of each month, don't pay all of your bills during the first week of the month and then file in the second week. Refrain from paying bills and stall creditors until the last possible date. When you have maximized the cash in your coffers, then you are ready to file. You will need money in the bank to survive a bankruptcy and the only way you can accumulate it is not to pay your creditors.

Work closely with your accounting staff and bankruptcy professionals to estimate the costs, including professional retainers for the first ninety days in bankruptcy. If you cannot build up a war chest of cash sufficient to last the first sixty to ninety days in bankruptcy, then you probably won't make it successfully through a chapter 11 reorganization.

Future Restrictions

There are only two legal restrictions after receiving a discharge from the bankruptcy court:

1. You are forbidden under the penalty of law to make any additional payments to any creditor whose debt was discharged by the bankruptcy.
2. If you were granted a chapter 7 discharge, you cannot petition the bankruptcy court for protection until six years have elapsed.*

*Bankruptcy is hardly a recent phenomenon and has its origins in the Bible (Deut. 14: 1–2 and Lev. 25: 2–10). The limitation of filing for bankruptcy only once every seven years also has its origins in the Bible, which declared every seventh year the sabbath or sabbatical year. During this special year most types of debts were nullified, indentured servants could voluntarily choose freedom, and the fields permitted to lay fallow to give them a rest.

Bankruptcy Terms

This section should help you understand the basic terminology used in bankruptcy.

The laws governing bankruptcy are called the *Bankruptcy Code*. The *U.S. district bankruptcy courts* administer the Bankruptcy Code under authority granted them by the U.S. circuit court of appeals for the district. The bankruptcy courts operate under the *Federal Rules of Bankruptcy Procedure*, which are commonly called the *bankruptcy rules*. Appeals from decisions of the bankruptcy court are heard by the *U.S. district court*.

When a debtor (or his attorney) voluntarily gives the petition for relief to the clerk of the bankruptcy court and receives a case number, the debtor has *filed* the petition.

Transactions involving the debtor and occurring before *filing the petition* and being granted an *order of relief* are *prepetition*. After receiving the case number, the transactions involving the debtor are termed *postpetition*.

An *involuntary* bankruptcy is where creditors petition the court for relief. The debtor or other parties in interest have the right to object to the petition, and no *order of relief* is granted to the petitioners until a hearing has been held and all creditors are notified.

Petitioners are debtors who file voluntary petitions. In an involuntary bankruptcy, the petitioners are the creditors who filed the petition.

Until the bankruptcy court says otherwise, upon receipt of the case number the debtor is entitled to an immediate *order for relief*. One part of this relief is the *automatic stay* protecting the debtor and his estate from most of the actions and proceedings initiated by *creditors* and those with *claims (claimants)*.

A *claim* is the right to receive a payment from the debtor. Not all claims are legally entitled under the Bankruptcy Code to receive payment.

A claim can be secured or unsecured, fixed or contingent, matured or unmatured, disputed or undisputed, or a judgment.

Claims against the estate and transactions involving the

debtor or the estate are categorized as either *prepetition* or *postpetition*. Another category, called *administrative claims*, is created during the pendency of the bankruptcy proceeding to pay fees and costs incurred by the bankruptcy.

A *creditor* is an entity that or individual who has a claim against the debtor that arose any time prior to the debtor filing the petition for relief.

All property of the debtor filing for bankruptcy, except those assets considered *exempt* under state and/or federal law, are considered the *bankrupt's estate*.

Prior to being granted a *discharge* from bankruptcy, the debtor is called a *bankrupt* and is in the *pendency of a bankruptcy proceeding*.

In a *liquidation*, the property of the bankrupt's estate is collected and liquidated for the benefit of the bankrupt's creditors.

In a *reorganization*, the bankrupt (or other interested party) must submit a *plan of reorganization* that must be *accepted* by the bankrupt's creditors and *confirmed* by the bankruptcy court or the appointed *trustee*.

In the *pendency of a bankruptcy proceeding*, the bankrupt's financial and business decisions affecting the *bankrupt's estate* are subject to the oversight of the bankruptcy court. The bankrupt must request written permission of the bankruptcy court (or the appointed trustee) to change the financial condition of the bankrupt estate, including permission to sell property, borrow money, or purchase on credit.

The debtor granted a *discharge* by the court is considered *discharged*. In a reorganization, the *bankrupt estate* continues to make payments to the creditors under the plan until a *final distribution* has been made. Following the final distribution the court enters a *final decree*. With the entry of the final decree, the court's authority over the former bankrupt is terminated.

Many legal terms, including *fraud, false pretenses,* and *alimony, maintenance, or child support,* have very specific definitions under the Bankruptcy Code that are different from other state and federal statutes. In a bankruptcy the definitions found in the Bankruptcy Code prevail.

Notes

1. See Bankruptcy Code, 11 U.S.C. § 523, for a complete listing of the ten types of debts excepted from discharge in bankruptcy.
2. Bankruptcy Code § 507 (2) (7) (7).
3. For additional definitions of bona fide disputes, see also In re *Reid*, 773 F.2d 945, 13 C.B.C.2d (MB) 781 (7th Cir. 1985), and *Rubin v. Belo Broadcasting Corp.*, 769 F.2d 611, 13 C.B.C.2d 599 (9th Cir. 1985).
4. Bankruptcy Code, 11 U.S.C. § 706(a).
5. Bankruptcy Code, 11 U.S.C. § 706(d).
6. Tom Furlong, "Swamped by Debtors and Abuse: The Southern California Bankruptcy System Is Struggling under a Deluge of Cases, Both Legitimate and Fraudulent," *Los Angeles Times*, January 12, 1992, p. A1.
7. Linda Greenhouse, "Court Expands Use of Chapter 11," *New York Times*, June 14, 1991, p. D1.
8. *Surviving Debt* (Boston: National Consumer Law Center, 1992), p. 230.
9. See Frederick W. Daly, *Stand Up to the IRS* (Berkeley, Calif.: Nolo Press, 1992), Chapter 11, for information and suggestions on dealing with the IRS on matters relating to past due trust fund taxes.
10. "I.R.S. Accord with Macy," *New York Times*, June 24, 1993, p. D17.
11. U.S. Senate Report No. 95-989, 95th Cong., 2d Sess. 88 (1978).
12. "Florida Is Gaining Reputation as Haven for Debtors Who Seek to Shelter Wealth," *Wall Street Journal*, August 3, 1990, p. B1.
13. T. Weidlich, "The Story Continues," *New York Law Journal*, January 18, 1993, p. 2.
14. *Wall Street Journal*, August 3, 1990.

12

Image And Communications

Communicate with Your Employees

Your company is a team, or at least it should function as one. As the team's quarterback you need to inform the team members about the current predicament of the company and what is required of each of them to win the game. You don't have to make the playoffs or the Super Bowl, but you don't want to place last in your league either.

When discussing the company's current situation with other managers and employees, don't hide the seriousness of the situation, but don't scare them with draconian predictions either.

Too often managers are observed trying to hide the major problems of the company from their staff until it was too late for the employees to work together as a team to gain any yardage on the field. Remember that no one likes to be surprised with adverse news.

Do not wait until the last minute to tell your staff that the company is experiencing troubles. Schedule a meeting or a series of meetings with your employees. Then prepare yourself for the meeting. Be positive, limit the surprises, and avoid attributing individual blame for the troubles. There is no advantage to be gained in blaming any one event or one person for the company's current troubles. Except for corporate responsibility for torts (wrongful acts) such as hazardous waste, medical products, foodstuffs, and product liabilities, it is rare that any one event can force a company into a situation of economic peril.

Be truthful and positive when meeting with your staff. It is appropriate to discuss the decline in the sales of your products and the high cost of operating the sales offices. However, it is inappropriate and imprudent to tell a group of employees that unless the situation improves, by the end of the month only half of them will have positions. It is also inappropriate to blame the troubles on the recently departed vice president of sales or the lousy computer system.

Cater your presentation to the level of the employees. Be direct and be clear about your objectives. Tell them what your role will be during the coming months and what each of them can do to help the company to survive and prosper.

Even in the shadow of a series of business defeats, always try to impart a positive and optimistic image. You are the leader and the team will rally around you. With proper motivation the team may take the ball further than you expect.

How to Tell the Staff about the Company's Troubles

1. Schedule the meeting for a morning in the early part of the week.
2. Provide doughnuts and coffee to set the stage for a friendly meeting.
3. Be prepared with an agenda. This is not an ad hoc meeting.
4. Remember to:
   • Be positive.
   • Cater your presentation to the level of the employees.
   • Be direct and be clear about your objectives.
   • Limit the surprises.
   • Avoid attributing individual blame for the troubles.
   • Be honest about the seriousness of the situation.
   • Avoid making draconian predictions.
5. Tell them:
   • Briefly how the company came to be in this position
   • What the company's game plan is for recovery

- What your role will be
- What each of them can contribute to help the company meet its objectives
6. Emphasize what you expect from each of them.
7. Assure them there is a light at the end of the tunnel.
8. Ask them for their input and **listen** to them.

Public Relations

Public relations (PR) is the external image that your company projects to the public. The company's external image may not resemble the true state of your company; it is the perceived truth about your company and its management. This image is more important during a troubled period than at any other time of your business history. *Do not ignore public relations.*

When experiencing financial troubles, expect that the world around you probably perceives your problems as even worse than they are. When laying off employees, expect that the public will think the company is on the verge of closing down all operations. When closing one or more locations, expect that the public will believe that the company is about to lay off all employees and terminate operations.

Managing PR is easy if the company plans for it. PR is almost impossible to manage if the company ignores it until a negative event happens.

Divide the public into three groups: (1) customers, (2) suppliers, and (3) the media. Each group is important and the company needs a different strategy for managing PR with each.

Communications in Troubled Times

The worst attitude to take is to become introverted and act like an ostrich, burying your head in the ground to hide from the world.

During troubled times you may often feel like saying, "Help! Stop the world: I want to get off!" But at all costs you must fight on.

The survival of your business depends on your ability
to keep your head when times get tough.

Customers

Customers are the company's lifeblood and are responsible for
furnishing it with a regular cash flow. Customers pay your salary and the company's rent. It is very important to keep them
happy. List the company's ten or twenty most important customers. Telephone each of them and arrange to have lunch or
to meet with them during the next few weeks.

If these customers see you in the flesh and hear from you,
they will be more likely to maintain a relationship with you. Be
honest with your customers. Don't pour out all of the company's
troubles, but let them know that you are experiencing difficulties. Work on getting the customers to believe that the company
will be in business for many years to come.

Don't mistake your customers for your friends. They are in
business to make money. They may be sympathetic to the company's plight, but they are more likely to do business with a
winner than with someone who may be a loser. Assure them
that the company is committed to winning.

Ask customers about their business. Let them tell you their
plans for the future, and ally yourself with their plans. How can
they not have confidence in a businessperson who has such a
strong interest in their future?

Listen to your customers' concerns about your business.
Why do they perceive the company as valuable to their future?
How could the company provide better service? If you were to
meet with them for lunch every month or two to review business, would it be helpful to them? Recognize your weaknesses,
be appreciative of any criticism offered, and ally yourself with
the value that the customer perceives in your business.

This is not the occasion to break new ground or to plant
new seeds. Don't push too hard for new sales from current customers. The objective of your lunch date is to maintain the customers' confidence and convince them of your ability to remain
a viable partner in their business.

Near the holiday season, on the anniversary of your starting the business, or on some other date of significance, it is beneficial to your public image to send greeting cards to your customers. Tell your customers you love them and add a personal note to as many cards as you can. If you can afford it, send small gifts to your customers as a token of your appreciation. Be conservative, not flashy. Nuts, candy, or fruit baskets are usually appreciated.

Don't forget to send thank you letters for renewals and new orders. These are the simple ways that you can let the customers know that their business is important to you. In a competitive marketplace, the personal approach may make the difference in maintaining customers' loyalty and patronage.

Suppliers

Relationships with suppliers are just as important as relationships with customers. Without products you have nothing to sell.

But suppliers don't just sell you a product. They can extend credit, speed up the delivery of special orders, accept returns, assist in disposing of excess inventory, and refer new customers. A good relationship with a supplier can stretch the company's cash flow, and a poor relationship can put it out of business.

The most important rule in managing relationships with suppliers is not to surprise them. Don't promise them payment when you know the company can't meet the commitment. If the company can't make an expected payment, then communicate, be reasonable, and negotiate with the supplier.

The Media

For the most part the media will ignore the company unless something catastrophic happens. It is good practice to have some contacts in the trade and local media. You don't want your layoff of twenty employees to be your first notice in the local press. Start today to have a positive presence in the media.

What Works

Press releases work. Simple, succinct notices sent to the local and industry press announcing good news about your company will be read and noticed. So issue press releases for upcoming events, new sales, big contracts, speaking engagements, awards received, promotions, expansions, and anniversaries. For speed, use a fax machine to distribute announcements to the media.

If you are contacted by the media for your comments on a news item, insist that any comments printed are attributed to you and printed verbatim. Many reporters write articles based entirely on an interview with one person without giving her credit. An inquiring reporter should be told that you are willing to speak with him if you receive credit. If he refuses tell him you are not interested.

When you receive recognition in the press, write the reporter and the editor and thank them. Let members of the media know whom they can contact with any questions about your company in the future. Send them complete information about your company for their files.

When your company receives recognition in the press, order professional reprints from the publisher. If you have camera-ready artwork, you can usually request these reprints with your logo, name, address, and telephone number on them. Send a copy of the reprint to every present, former, and potential future customer and to the company's suppliers.

What Doesn't Work

Don't treat reporters and editors to a free lunch or a drink—it usually doesn't work. If the news about your company is significant enough, they will cover the story. And if it isn't, a free lunch won't make a difference.

Be Prepared for the Media

Whatever happens, do not be caught unprepared for the media. You do not want to be in a response mode when members of

terminate the other voice numbers and fax numbers, and have a recording installed stating the equivalent telephone numbers at the new location.

Media Announcements

The local media may or may not take notice of a closing. It usually depends on whether there is more significant news that week. It may be to the advantage of the company's public image to send a brief press release to the local media about the company's decision with the appropriate reasons to maintain a positive image.

Exhibit 12-2 is an example of a press release that announces the closing of two unprofitable locations of a laundry and drycleaning business and maintains a positive image. The press release maintains a positive image by calling the closing a "consolidation" and headlines the closing by announcing the expansion of facilities at the main (and now the only) location. The business has done little "expansion" to the main facility except for relocating two counter clerks from the locations to be closed to handle the additional volume, but the press release is entirely truthful. The impression that is left with the reader is not one of a troubled business but of a business undergoing *expansion* to provide *improved service.*

Notes

1. Helen Huntley, "Eckerd to Eliminate 600 Jobs," *St. Petersburg Times,* August 5, 1992.
2. Elliot Zweibach, "250 Positions Eliminated as Safeway Restructures," *Supermarket News,* March 8, 1993.
3. Karen Alexander, "Fluke to Restructure Operations," *Seattle Times,* November 20, 1992.
4. "Business Changes Force Lockheed to Lay Off 500," *PR Newswire,* November 5, 1992.

13
Who Can Assist You

During troubled times business owners and principals often go to great lengths to stay alive. Their actions are not always prudent. They clutch at straws, mortgage their future, take counsel from pretenders, and refuse counsel from sages. Who can forget automobile manufacturer John De Lorean's involvement with a cocaine deal, not to use the profits for his own personal benefit, but to keep the automobile company that bore his name alive and producing vehicles.

The cast of characters that descends upon a troubled company is a motley crew of financial players: vultures, loan brokers, middlemen, "1-percenters," opportunists, and creative financiers. Most of these players are opportunists and very few have ever successfully helped a company in trouble. Mostly what they do is raise your hopes and waste your time, and if you are foolish enough to pay their expenses, they'll spend your money, too.

These birds of prey can carry business cards of reputable companies but explain to you that your type of deal is one that they "need to handle on the side" or that they "can't handle it but have a friend who for 1 percent can arrange an introduction. . . ." Some of these birds are convicted felons, con artists, and confidence men. Most work out of the front seat of their car or another person's office. Don't waste your time with these vultures.

One simple way to sift the wheat from the chaff is to ask all "professionals" for references from businesses that they have "assisted" in the past year. Most are unable to provide any references. If someone does give you names, then carefully check the references and maybe, just maybe, you have found a person who can help you.

There are those whose advice you may want to consider and those that you will have to consider. As a troubled company you may need lawyers, accountants, and turnaround consultants as traveling companions on the road to recovery.

Lawyers

The troubled company needs legal assistance during the process of recovery, but be wary of using lawyers for business counsel. You wouldn't go to your dentist for advice on a sprained wrist, nor should you ask your legal counsel to be your business consultant.

You need advice from a lawyer who has experience in very specific areas of the law. Most debtor/creditor relationships and remedies are governed by state law, therefore, be certain that your counsel is well versed and experienced in debtor/creditor law in the primary state that you operate in.

A lawyer is only a good tool when utilized properly. Never forget that the lawyer is your servant. He works on your behalf. If a lawyer will not act upon your instructions, you may have to fire him.

Before choosing a lawyer, we strongly suggest you read about one of the most shameful examples of lawyers running amok in Sol Stein's *Bankruptcy: A Feast for Lawyers*.[1] Stein describes some of the problems that he encountered during the chapter 11 bankruptcy filing of the publishing company that bore his name, Stein & Day.

Lawyers in small communities can easily have conflicts of interest when dealing with your creditors. If the attorney or her law firm represents or is under retainer to any of your creditors, she may be prohibited from representing you. To make the process efficient, show the attorney the list of your creditors and ask her if she has any conflicts of interest before discussing the merits and the details of your case.

Don't let your lawyer become an angry creditor. Work out a

plan for the payment of his services. Avoid personally guaranteeing payment for the lawyer's services. All business is conducted with some amount of risk. Lawyers would like you to believe that they conduct business without the same risk as your other vendors. This is a myth and you shouldn't believe it.

Clearly document all instructions that you give to counsel. Confirm all telephone conversations in writing and fax copies to your counsel. Instruct your counsel that you *require* copies of all letters, court documents, pleadings, and memoranda sent or written on your company's behalf.

Trust your lawyer as a business associate with the role of providing legal counsel and advice. Never consider your lawyer to be your partner because he is only your partner until you owe him money. Then he can become your worst creditor.

See Chapter 11 for a detailed discussion of choosing counsel when contemplating the option of bankruptcy.

Accountants

Your current accountant may or may not be qualified to give you advice when you are facing economic troubles or possible insolvency. Many of the same rules that apply to legal counsel apply to accountants.

The accountant's code of ethics is much less strict than that of your legal counsel and the information you or others in your company impart to the accountant is not protected by the lawyer/client privilege. Do not confide in your accountant as you would your lawyer.

If you need to choose a new accountant with expertise in insolvency and bankruptcy, then do so without hesitation. Nothing prevents a company from having relationships with more than one firm of accountants. There is nothing wrong with using different tools to accomplish different tasks.

Many an accountant would like to play lawyer or management consultant, but you should be skeptical of those who try to wear too many hats. Some accountants are excellent management consultants, and some have more background and experience in the laws surrounding insolvency than your own lawyer.

Therefore, listen to their ideas—but be wary of taking their advice before checking with your own legal counsel.

Turnaround Consultants

Consultants who bridge the gap between a company's management, creditors, lawyers, and accountants can be invaluable to the troubled company. Look for those who specialize in workouts, insolvency, business turnarounds, and debt restructuring.

Why do you need a turnaround consultant? There are a number of reasons:

- *Experience.* They are experienced at managing companies in a crisis. They know what to expect and have solutions to the everyday problems of distressed companies.
- *Focus.* Their only job is the survival and resurrection of your business.
- *Time.* They give you time to do the things you need to do. Even if you were able to make all of the correct decisions in a turnaround, you are unlikely to be able to do it and simultaneously manage the company.
- *New blood.* They provide someone else for your creditors to talk to. Creditors will listen to experts who have successfully effected other workouts and arranged satisfactory payouts for creditors.
- *Contacts.* They know the best lawyers and accountants for assisting with a successful turnaround.

Unlike accountants and lawyers, turnaround consultants are not bound by any formal code of ethics. This can be an advantage. However, remember that nothing you tell the consultant is protected by the attorney/client privilege, and this can be a disadvantage.

Negotiate a fee structure with consultants that rewards them for their performance without placing them on a precipice when advising you. Consultants should be paid on a per day or per week basis, with a bonus based on meeting specific objectives. Some contingent fee structure is recommended, but don't put the majority of their compensation out on the limb until you are 100 percent certain of the course you intend to take.

General Rules for Managing Relationships with Professionals (e.g., Accountants, Lawyers, Consultants, and Loan Brokers)

1. Require that all professionals execute an engagement agreement that includes protection for confidentiality, nondisclosure, and noncircumvention before undertaking the assignment.
2. Use the professional only for his specialty. Don't try to use a hammer to do the job of a screwdriver.
3. Be ever vigilant of and conscious of conflicts of interest.
4. Confirm all instructions and understandings in writing. Use your fax machine to confirm and to acknowledge meetings and telephone calls.
5. Keep copies of all documents and correspondence sent to professionals. Stamp dates and times on all documents.
6. Don't permit the professional to become an angry creditor. She knows too much about your business and could mortally wound you with her inside knowledge.
7. Know the professional's code of ethics. Most will ignore it; you should not.
8. The professionals are not your friends. They are in business to make a profit. They will remain sympathetic only as long as you are paying for their services. It's cheaper to use a psychiatrist than a business professional for a shoulder to cry upon.
9. Question their invoices. Insist upon detailed billing; it may help to keep them honest.
10. Negotiate a fee structure in advance. Include a bonus or contingent fee where appropriate and permitted.

Note

1. Sol Stein, *Bankruptcy: A Feast for Lawyers*, 2nd ed. (New York: M. Evans & Co., 1992).

14

Security and The Troubled Company

Although security should always be an important concern for management, a troubled company must be extra careful to avoid any significant losses of material assets or information. Security breaches such as fraud, theft, and leaks of confidential information that are merely harmful to a healthy company can be fatal to a troubled company.

Many experts believe that corporate America remains oblivious to the real depth of the problem of security in the workplace. A troubled company cannot afford to ignore this risk. Security problems are like cancers. If left undetected, they can grow and fester for years before becoming fatal to their host. Management is often naive when it comes to the area of security. Even when confronted with irrefutable evidence that other companies in its industry have been ripped off or compromised, management repeatedly denies that it is happening to its company.

A troubled company can use many techniques to safeguard its business and property from harm. Although nothing management can do will result in a 100 percent secure business, a program of increased security will reduce and control the losses. These savings can mean the difference between the success and failure of a turnaround mission.

Types of Security Breaches

Fraud

Fraud, embezzlement, and kickbacks cost North American businesses more than $27 billion in 1993, and some experts believe the figure is even higher because most companies are too embarrassed to report internal wrongdoing or simply never see it. Estimates of the annual cost of telecommunications fraud alone in the United States range from $1 billion to as much as $9 billion.

Theft

The annual cost of theft to American retail and wholesale business, according to experts, ranges from a low estimate of about $60 billion to a high of about $100 billion. *No business can succeed when its assets are being stolen, least of all a troubled business.*

Particularly in a distressed company, where workers are insecure about jobs and the company's commitment to them, workplace ethics have been eroded. Employees rationalize thefts while still seeing themselves as the good guys and the employer as the bad guy. Even when caught in the act, employees rationalize their behavior with excuses of low pay and "everyone does it," according to Joe Mele, loss prevention specialist with the National Crime Prevention Institute at the University of Louisville in Kentucky.[1]

Leaks of Confidential Information

Most incidents of corporate espionage go undetected, and even those that are detected are often sheltered from publicity. "It is really quite common," says Richard Heffernan, a leading security expert and a consultant to the FBI on industrial espionage. "Most executives feel this is something that happens in a movie or to someone else, and really it is happening on a regular basis to a large number of corporations."[2]

All companies are potentially at risk of corporate spying, but high-technology companies, companies bringing new products to market, and those with highly regarded customers have the highest risk.

Security expert Peter Schweizer, in his recent book *Friendly Spies*, estimates that American companies lose $100 billion annually to industrial espionage.[3] This is more likely to happen in troubled companies as workers look to gain an edge in the search for future employment. Everyone from GM to IBM has been hurt by losses due to thefts of corporate secrets.

The Evil That Lurks Within

Although police experts have estimated that almost two-thirds of all crime against businesses are committed by their own employees, many companies are still reluctant to admit they have a problem. Management will go to great lengths to protect the business from external threats without addressing the potential and real threat that lurks within. *Only through the education of employees at all levels of the company can the attitudes about crime in the workplace be changed.*

A Reluctance to Prosecute

Many companies that discover criminal activity from within are reluctant to prosecute because of their fear of adverse publicity and embarrassment. The "embarrassment syndrome" can become systemic to a company and thwart management's efforts to prevent and control future security problems.

Employees don't want to "rat" on other employees. Managers don't want to report their observations of employee dishonesty to corporate executives, and the executives don't want to alarm directors and shareholders, etc. This philosophy of denying and obscuring the true magnitude of the problem persists into the annual reports of most publicly held companies.

When was the last time you heard a company publicly admit that it had a problem with crime? Instead of telling their shareholders they have a problem with theft, companies simply add a category to their financial statements euphemistically called "shrinkage" to accommodate any unexplained changes (thefts) of inventory.[4]

Why You Should Prosecute Dishonest Employees

Saying that a certain amount of crime is acceptable is a myth that mangers would like to hide behind. When a troubled company is laying off employees and reducing benefits, no amount of "shrinkage" or "slippage" is acceptable or should be permitted. If management does look the other way, it should not be a surprise, according to loss prevention specialist Joe Mele, that thefts by employees will rise to the highest level that management is willing to accept.[5]

Employers must work with their employees, in a team effort, to combat crime. *The primary reason for pursuing convictions against perpetrators is the deterrent effect that it has upon others and the support that it provides to honest employees.*

What the Troubled Company Can Do about Crime

The methods for combating crime are the same for healthy or troubled companies. The only difference is that while a healthy company may be able to withstand a few battlefield defeats before eventually winning the war, a troubled company may bleed to death for lack of staying power.

Education, Prevention, and Control

The troubled company's arsenal of weapons in the war against crime can be referred to as EPC: Education, Prevention, and Control.[6]

Education

There are three aspects of education:

1. Employees must be educated that crimes against the company are hazardous to the company's financial health and are everyone's concern.

- Receive an excessive amount of telephone messages or personal mail
- Appear to be making unusual requests for office supplies or equipment
- Refuse to take vacations for fear of what might be revealed in their absence

Prevent the problem from spreading by limiting access to the facilities after hours and by being vigilant in looking for theft of company assets. And control the problem by prosecuting all offenders and implementing a zero tolerance policy for all theft.

> We often discover employees typing résumés, job applications, or academic term papers for friends after hours using company word processors. Even if the employee charges the friend for the service, this is not the type of business that requires harsh actions (unless done on company time). A reminder to employees to be judicious in their use of company resources and not to let it interfere with company business or be done during company time is usually sufficient to limit the practice.

Using Private Security

Don't use outside security companies as replacements for proper security procedures, but retain them to help your company to do risk assessment and construct a plan for risk management. The plan should include recommendations on education, prevention, and control of security risks.

Private security companies can provide a variety of services to the troubled company including: background checks; corporate security reviews; criminal investigations; investigations into financial fraud, industrial problems, insurance fraud, and machinery malfunctions; photography; polygraph tests; premises surveillance; protection; risk assessment; risk management; security guards; surveillance; warranty fraud; and workers compensation liability investigations.

When choosing a security company, get good references. It is useful if the security company has experience in your industry, but it is not essential. It doesn't matter if the business is a furrier or a bookstore—a warehouse is a warehouse.

Establish clear and concise objectives for security consultants. Tell them what you want from them and have them make a proposal. Get competitive bids from several companies and select the one most responsive to your needs.

If you need to hire security guards, be certain that the company trains all of its guards and has the resources necessary to manage them.

EPC Reviewed

Managers should use a combination of EPC—education, prevention, and control—to create a secure environment in which to conduct business.

Stopping illegal activity isn't a matter of more expensive technology to scrutinize every activity in the business. Preventing and controlling illegal activity requires well-designed management practices, close management and employee cooperation, professional assistance, and—most importantly—educational awareness of the problem.

Don't ignore the issue of security until after you suffer a loss. A troubled company can easily be mortally wounded by only one or two small losses.

Don't think that security is something that only healthy companies can afford. Good security is not expensive, but it does require a change in attitude and a regular program of education.

If you need to employ security professionals, then don't hesitate. Since you probably can't afford the costs of the losses, you can't afford not to hire professionals to assist in designing a program of prevention and control.

Practice EPC every day and for every new project. Make a security risk assessment a requirement for every new project. The same way a budget is designed for every project, a security program must be incorporated.

Notes

1. Judith Egerton, "Employee Theft on the Rise," *Louisville Courier Journal*, October 30, 1992.
2. David Schwab, "Loose Lips Could Sink Firm's Profits: Corporate Espionage on Rise," *Plain Dealer*, February 24, 1993, p. G3.
3. See Peter Schweizer, *Friendly Spies* (New York: Atlantic Monthly Press, 1993) for an excellent account of the depth of corporate espionage by French, Japanese, and Israeli interests aimed at gaining economic advantage over the United States. After reading this book, many corporate executives will be loath to leave their briefcases unattended while in a foreign country or to give a factory tour to foreign "specialists."
4. E. J. Muller, "How to Cope with Theft and Drugs: Warehouse Theft and Workplace," *Distribution*, November 1991, p. 84.
5. Egerton.
6. Susan M. Werner, "Ask a Risk Manager: Holiday Pressures Spur Violence in the Workplace," *Business Insurance*, December 14, 1992, p. 19.

15

Some Final Thoughts

As the American economy shows new signs of life and rebirth in the mid-1990s, there will be the ever-present threat of returning to the glorious days of the "growth for its own sake" management styles of the 1980s. The sharp improvements in profitability, productivity, and competitiveness show that management is capable of achieving more and better with less in the 1990s. The style of virtual or hollow organizations operating with 75 percent of their previous management force will remain meaningful for years to come. This is especially true in an economy based on competitiveness, being a low-cost producer or retailer, and leading through innovation.

The process of economic and managerial transformation of the early 1990s has shown us that most of the concepts we espoused in the 1970s and 1980s about human resources were not efficient or effective. Excess perks and rewards produced a management that became lazy and unmotivated. The human resources dominance of the management process over leader ship strategy and common sense produced bloated bureaucracies that were anti-entrepreneurial and incapable of managing change.

Everyone had a title. Secretaries became administrative assistants and everyone else was a coordinator, a term commonplace in the stagnant bureaucracy. But no one seemed responsible for getting things done.

Management guru Peter Drucker wrote about the need to ensure that "responsibility should always exceed authority."

Index